EMPATH

A Survival Guide for Highly Sensitive People

(The Science of Highly Sensitive People –
Master Your Personality)

Gloria Perkins

Published By Gloria Perkins

Gloria Perkins

All Rights Reserved

Empath: A Survival Guide for Highly Sensitive People (The Science of Highly Sensitive People – Master Your Personality)

ISBN 978-1-77485-410-5

All rights reserved. No part of this guide may be reproduced in any form without permission in writing from the publisher except in the case of brief quotations embodied in critical articles or reviews.

Legal & Disclaimer

The information contained in this book is not designed to replace or take the place of any form of medicine or professional medical advice. The information in this book has been provided for educational and entertainment purposes only.

The information contained in this book has been compiled from sources deemed reliable, and it is accurate to the best of the Author's knowledge; however, the Author cannot guarantee its accuracy and validity and cannot be held liable for any errors or omissions. Changes are periodically made to this book. You must consult your doctor or get professional medical advice before using any of the suggested remedies, techniques, or information in this book.

Upon using the information contained in this book, you agree to hold harmless the Author from and against any damages, costs, and expenses, including any legal fees potentially resulting from the application of any of the information provided by this guide. This disclaimer applies to any damages or injury caused by the use and application, whether directly or indirectly, of any advice or information presented, whether for breach of contract, tort, negligence, personal injury, criminal intent, or under any other cause of action.

You agree to accept all risks of using the information presented inside this book. You need to consult a professional medical practitioner in order to ensure you are both able and healthy enough to participate in this program.

TABLE OF CONTENTS

INTRODUCTION 1

CHAPTER 1: DEFINITION OF EMPATHY 10

CHAPTER 2: A COMPLETE GUIDE FOR PSYCHOMETRY AND PSYCHIC ABLITIES 23

CHAPTER 3: WHAT EMPATH PEOPLE ARE (THE COMMON PERSONALITY AND THE THINGS THEY FEAR) 43

CHAPTER 4: DEALING WITH ENERGY VAMPIRES 55

CHAPTER 5: THE COMPREHENSIVE GUIDE TO PSYCHOMETRY 74

CHAPTER 6: SPIRITUAL HYPERSENSITIVITY AND EMPATHS 93

CHAPTER 7: HOW TO PROTECT YOURSELF FROM ENERGY VAMPIRES 99

CHAPTER 8: TIPS TO MANAGE YOUR EMPATHY WITHOUT GETTING TIRED 110

CHAPTER 9: WHAT IS IT MEAN TO BE AN EMPATH? 116

CHAPTER 10: TIPS FOR ENDURANCE FOR EMPATHS, HIGHLY SENSITIVE AND HIGHLY SENSITIVE PEOPLE 136

CHAPTER 11: HOW TO MAKE USE OF ESSENTIAL OILS AND AROMATHERAPY TO HELP HIGHLY SENSITIVE PEOPLE .. 150

CHAPTER 12: TELEPATHY 155

CHAPTER 13: ABUSE OF EMOTIONS IS NOT OK HOW TO IDENTIFY AND PROTECT YOURSELF FROM THIS ABUSE. 174

CONCLUSION.. 182

Introduction

An empath is a person who is deeply sensitive to the feelings and emotions of all those in their vicinity. The ability to perceive what other people are feeling is beyond compassion (characterized by the capacity to feel the feelings of other people) and extends to truly take those feelings to heart; experiencing the feelings of another in a way that is passionate.

It is a fact that scientists have discovered the concept of "mirror neurons" within the brain which could assist us in reflecting the emotions of people who we come in contact with. It also suggests that certain people may be more likely to have mirror neurons than the rest, suggesting that empaths exist.

There's no doubt that some people are more inclined to be compassionate than other. We've all had someone that was proficient at reading our thoughts similar to how we've encountered people who appear to be completely disconnected from the feelings of others around them.

Empathy is an accepted trait that exists across a spectrum, with some people being extremely compassionate, and others (insane people) without compassion entirely. How do you measure your empathy? And, what point would you consider your own self to be an empath?

The most efficient method to determine if You're an Empath

Start by asking yourself a couple of questions regarding how you relate to people around you and how you really and honestly react to huge joyful events that occur within your own personal life. If you can respond "yes" to a majority of these questions There's a good chance you're an empath.

Do you ever find yourself becoming a victim to pressures of others?

Are you being blamed for being overly sensitive before?

Do you feel overwhelmed in crowded spaces?

Do you think that others will portray you as compassionate?

Diverse empathy specialists offer their own tests to aid you in determining if you're an empath yourself. Dr. Dr. Judith Orloff asks "Do I often feel like I'm not a part of the community?" While self-declared empath Tara Merrick-Robson asks if you have trouble watching the news or notice the poor motion pictures that are overwhelming.

Benefits and drawbacks of being an Empath

Let's look at some of the advantages and drawbacks from becoming an empath.

Pros

*You can be a source of enthusiastic support for others

You know when someone needs assistance

* You can discern you if you will gain from someone who will benefit you.

Cons

You may feel frequently exhausted

It is possible to think that it's difficult to find the perfect opportunity for you

* Your ability to browse other profiles might be viewed as intrusive by some

Experts

There are certain advantages of being an empath. If you have the ability to take advantage of the feelings of those around you, you should also be able to better assist and help those that matter to you the most.

Recognizing that someone else may be experiencing sadness, despair or scared, irrespective whether they're able to seem to be displaying it, puts you in the position of being able to assist the person through it, gaining their trust and proving to be someone they can be able to rely on in the future.

This makes you a better partner and companion, and could aid in strengthening your connections all the time.

Being so adjusted also means you'll need to spot a fraud ahead of time. Empaths shouldn't have to worry about being manipulated due to the fact that they're not easily deceived or controlled. Furthermore, if they are, it's because they didn't realize their true feelings regarding someone else and not because of the fact that they missed the warning signs out and about.

Cons

There are, of course, susceptible to some real damage to being associated with other people's feelings. A majority of the writing on empaths advises that they can be easily overwhelmed when in crowded spaces or during events that are genuinely charged (like funerals and weddings) because they absorb the sentiments of those around them as if they were an ointment. It's not hard to imagine the speed at which this could become extremely debilitating in particular settings.

It can be difficult for empaths who are prone to apathy in the event that they're constantly expressing their feelings to other people. They may struggle to rest or maintain their psychological health in the event they aren't able to figure out how to alter the information sources that they're constantly receiving.

There could be some people who are unsure of the way you seem to be able to understand them. There are many people who need to be a breeze to read, and if you keep the fact that while you could think that you are trying to helpothers, some might be able to see your emotions and thoughts to be intrusive and unwelcome.

Be Sure to Protect Yourself In the Event of an Empath

In the event that you're a fan of an empath and if you are constantly taking on the emotions of others, it's essential to determine how to protect your mind and keep yourself away from the the world in order to take a breath, repair the wounds, and be able to experience your own emotions.

Plan out the Time For Yourself

This could involve finding a way to get away from any help offered by others in nature and not be constantly bombarded by another's thoughts or worries. However, it could mean locating music or a schedule of reflection which will assist you in setting up and resetting your center once again.

Empaths should also take a look at how and when to build distinct dividers within themselves with the intention that they're not successfully retaining the emotions of others who is around them. It's not easy and establishing limits isn't a simple task for empaths that are inclined to assist. However setting up limits is crucial for everyone's emotional wellbeing and well-being, perhaps especially for empaths.

You may need to start by practicing reflection in order to determine the best way to accomplish this. By focusing your mind and working out ways to shut out interruptions from outside and then increase your ability to perform the same when the enthralling information you get from others can be extraordinary.

Choose Carefully Whom You Spend your time with

It's also possible to learn over time that there are certain individuals who you're in a good position to be able to separate yourself from. Because empaths take in the feelings of others, putting lots of energy in people who are poisonous could cause you to harm you from the back to the front.

There are certain groups that you aren't able to help while there are others that you're in a perfect situation to avoid - that's fine. Understanding that, and recognizing your personal limits is among the optimal way to protect your mental well-being and health.

In the end, searching for help from experts is not an unwise option. In the event that you feel constantly overwhelmed or exhausted from the emotions you experience when you step out of your front door it is possible to make use of a few tools to assist you in overcoming those feelings.

A trained psychological health expert will assist you in fostering the tools that will make it possible for you to become the most joyous, most positive version of yourself you can be.

There, you will be able to discover how you can make use of the empath abilities of yours once you possess the speed of transfer that you are able to assist and focus on the people who need it the most.

Chapter 1: Definition Of Empathy

Empathy could be a word which is frequently used without having a clear idea of what it entails or what it means in the context of a real-world application. There are times when you'll see this word being applied in a way which isn't in accordance with the person's beliefs and values. This is why it's of paramount importance that we determine what empathy is and how you can recognize it in your daily life.

The easiest way to test the depth of empathy you have is place yourself in the position of someone who is not you. This means that you're able to comprehend how someone is experiencing and what they're doing. But this isn't always the easiest method to test.

It could be that certain people are more easily empathetic than others. Most of the time, this is due to the nature of these people having been through a lot of life events. They are able to see the struggle in pain and suffering that others are experiencing.

Imagine it along these guidelines:

If you know someone who has lost parents, you'll instantly connect with them, especially if you've suffered the loss parents you know. You'll be able to relate to the things they're doing and give them your own perspective. However, if you've not experienced this loss for yourself and you're not familiar with the grieving process, it's more difficult for you to gain an understanding of the grief of the person.

It's important to remember that it's not necessary for you to go through the same journey in order to feel empathy for anyone. It's a myth that tends to pervade the thoughts of the majority of people. However, it's definitely more attainable to relate to someone else's experience when you're in exactly the same circumstance.

Additionally, having experienced an similar experience can lead to empathy to be an experience of bonding. For instance, in the military soldiers are quick to bond when they realize that they've had similar experiences. They may not have fought in the same conflict or even been part of the same unit, but being having similar experiences that lets them be connected and bond at a similar level.

However, being empathic does not mean you must go through every type of feeling in the world. The fact of the issue is that we all have the same emotions: grief, sadness, happiness sadness, and so on. Also, becoming an extremely sensitive person is a skill that you could learn. This isn't something that we're all born with, and that's the reason. It's a quality that needs time to identify and to grow. Naturally, some people naturally have more empathy than others. However, everyone is able to develop empathy skills.

That's why the remarks of ex- US president Barack Obama eloquently illustrate this idea: "Learning to face in the shoes of someone else to see the world through their eyes is how peace starts. It's your responsibility to make that happen. Empathy can be a trait of character that can change our world".

From this great statement, we can learn a lot.

The first step is to learn to view the world from the eyes of someone else. Once you've learned to view the world from another's viewpoint, you'll be able to be able to take on the shoes of someone else. It's now very simple for you to transform into another person who thinks the same to what you're doing. However, once you start to see the world by looking through the eyes of someone who thinks differently to the way to you, then you're beginning to truly become an empath.

If you're willing to look at the world by the lens of adversaries, you'll be that much more sympathetic. You'll certainly see the world in the eye of adversaries however that doesn't mean you've to be in agreement with them. However, being able to determine where your adversaries come from is an excellent way will allow you to defuse potential violent situations.

Think about this illustration.

It is inevitable to head to be promoted. In this sense, this person is your opponent. You both desire the job as much as you can and will do anything to get you to be there. You work within the timeframe and have your jobs completed.

Your boss then decides to award a promotion your coworker. If you're not a sympathetic person, you could be angry and bitter at the way this person got the job over you. You're taking this choice personally and deciding to take to take it out on others around you. This negative response results in an eroding of your performance , which could put your job at risk.

In contrast, you decide to alter the script and approach this match from the viewpoint of your colleague. You see an impressive adversary in you, but they require to work hard because they have families to take care of. Therefore, the increase they receive from their promotion will go a long way to providing food for their family and helping to pay for the bills at home.

When your boss informs you that your colleague got the promotion they worked for, to earn it, and their family members will appreciate the boost in salary. In addition, you could be happy for the person you work with since they got it the promotion fair and even.

If you can show that your colleague received the job promotion through thwarting your efforts or committing a shady act, then you have every right to express your displeasure. In these instances, there is no need to accept any dishonesty from anyone.

You'll notice that an compassionate person looks at the world from the other person's viewpoint and experiences things deeply and isn't afraid to speak and doesn't take anything personally. Even though an empathetic individual isn't a slave in any way, they're able to feel , and not react as an automated.

The famous American writer Maya Angelou once said "I believe we all share empathy. It's just that we don't have enough confidence to show it". The words are relevant because of the desire to show our feelings in the the circumstances which others are facing. We'll see suffering and injustice wherever we are. We may feel pity for those who suffer, but we're not always the will to do take action to alleviate the situation. Of course , there are instances in which we are unable to accomplish anything. In these situations, it's better to take a step back and let those who are able to perform something, do it. We'd be more than willing to assist by helping those who can make a difference important in this circumstance.

Perhaps you're worried about by a natural catastrophe which has devastated the country far away. Although it's impossible to get on a plane to help, you can help those who are making a contribution in any way contribute to organizations that are able to help the people who are in need.

Another example of this is in the animal enthusiasts. They are empathetic for animals who are lost or stray however they have the ability to adopt every animal that is injured or lost. Therefore, they donate to the local animal shelter in whatever way they can. It is not necessary to give huge sums of money. Just a few hours of volunteering every opportunity you have can make an impact.

On the other hand of the spectrum, you'll demonstrate your compassion for others by not doing anything. In this case, you're focused about being environmentally conscious and be willing to help callers in any means you can. You're trying to avoid from engaging in activities that hurt the environment. Also, you want to take an active role in recycling and reducing energy use and in educating others on ways to assist the environment.

These are just a few examples of ways you can aid a cause that is more important from your particular corner of the globe. It's not necessary to become a spokesperson for an issue or take on an action. You can lead a life that is transformative simply by engaging in the kinds of behaviors and actions that can be accumulated over time. This attitude starts with your capacity to distinguish what's going on from the perspective of other people. If you're an unpalatable person, you'll do everything to make your case even if that it involves destroying other people. You don't care the way others browse as long since you're happy and content.

It's true that selfish people live miserable lives since they must feed on other people to further their own agenda. Empathic people live happier and more fulfilling lives since they're willing to give back to the world by their actions.

Empathetic people usually are a symbol of something and adhere to beliefs that resonate to their personal views of the world. But they're also ready to consider these values and turn around to determine how they stack up in the minds of other people. An empathic person also is able to see the world by looking at it from a different perspective, even although they may not necessarily agree the views of that person.

Another important thing to be considered in this chapter is there is a difference between sympathy and empathy. Although empathy is an intense feeling of sensitivity to the feelings of others , sympathy could be a superficial emotion that only acknowledges the pain other people go through.

Being sympathetic, however, only does little to improve a situation. This is why it's normal to hear people say "oh it's terrible" however they look around and do not act on it. Being empathetic does not obligate you to be empathetic, it does take you to the point in which the other person is standing.

Additionally, sympathy is frequently mistaken for condescendence. If people behave in such a manner, they'll appear to be on the higher moral level. They can even be judgmental, especially when they think that someone's bad luck is due to the actions of their personal. For instance, these people see those who are in tough economic times because of losing their job. They'll say "that isn't easy. Being fired is typically hard". This type of assertion hardly reflect the character of someone who is very compassionate. It is usually an acknowledgement of a difficult circumstance. Sometimes, condescension can be a factor when someone states something like "how horrible! I could not think of going through the motions of losing my job!"

In this sentence, it appears that this person is claiming an ethical stand by in which they say "I have a fantastic job but I am not sure how I could do to change the situation since I'm extremely fortunate not to lose work".

It's true that a highly compassionate person could shut down and refrain from saying anything that could be misinterpreted (especially when they are unable to understand the circumstance) or say an expression like "that's rough. I can remember a time when I was fired from my job. ..."

This is a clear indication of the way an empathic person will respond. In the end, they must have had a personal experience in the same circumstance or be able to relate to the situations individuals are looking at. Empathy involves placing yourself out there and exposing your vulnerability. It is difficult to admit that you also are in the same pain and suffering.

In the same way, it's difficult to be happy for someone other than the need to boast about your achievements. Because of this, empathetic people have experienced, it is not uncommon for the address of someone else's is placed in the spotlight.

They'll be able to understand why because they have been in the spotlight as well.

If you believing that empathy is suppressing your own feelings for the sake of others, then you'd prefer to focus on this: we're all equally valuable. There instances when other people's requirements are more important than our own. You'll understand that when you're in a position to comprehend what others see in their own eyes.

Chapter 2: A Complete Guide For Psychometry And Psychic Ablities

In short it is the process by which an individual can easily comprehend or "read" the history of an object by touching it. The person can either place it on their forehead or place it in their palms. Every touch makes them feel something regarding the item. These impressions may take the form of smells, sounds images, feelings, or even taste.

What exactly is Psychometry?

Psychometry is a unique skill by which people are able to learn to perceive things that aren't visible within the world. It is sometimes described as the ability to see with a psychic perspective. Different people see in different ways. Certain people see through the surface of black glass, water or a crystal ball every person has their own method. The most distinctive feature for psychometry lies in the fact that you are able to practice this amazing ability by using their hands.

Someone with psychometric abilities is usually called a psychometrist. As an example, let's say you gift them an old watch and they put this in their hand. They could tell you everything about the watch and the person who was the owner using their ability to touching. They can even inform you about various things that happened when the watch owner was wearing the watch. Naturally psychics can provide you with different information and give you some insight into what the owner of the item was like, the things they did throughout their lives or even when they passed away. However, among all these possibilities, the primary aspect that psychics are able to provide is the way the person in question was feeling at a particular point in the time in their lives. There is a belief that objects are able to very effectively keep a person's emotions within it, and, consequently, psychometrics can detect the emotions of a person very quickly.

It's important to note that a psychometric might not be able to demonstrate the same level of reading or seeing with different objects. The precision of their abilities to read between one object and the next. The majority of people are not aware of the fundamental concept behind psychometry. It isn't focused on the future , but the present and the past. This is why it differs from a normal read from a crystal ball.

The idea of psychometry as well as the term itself was invented by Joseph Rhodes Buchanan, an American doctor, physiologist and physician. He explained psychometry by using geologists as an example. Similar to geologists who study the past through fossils, psychometry is linked to mental fossils.' The objects emit particular energy that can be used to study the history and science of human brain.

Psychometrists, in essence, are of the opinion that every thing on earth has a soul, which includes objects. They develop a memory depending on how an individual interacts with them. It is possible to determine the story behind the object or the owner of it If they have the ability to sense the energy that emanates from the objects.

A Short History of Psychometry

In the year 1842 Joseph R. Buchanan was the first person to coin the term "psychometry.' The term is derived from two Greek words: metron and psyche. The word psyche translates to'soul metron refers to "measurement.' Of all the studies that were conducted using psychometry Buchanan is among the pioneers to use it. Buchanan was an American professor of physiology. At first, he stored different kinds of substances inside glass bottles. Following that, he enlisted his students to grasp the vials to determine the kinds of drugs that have been stored in them through the effect of touching. It was more than luck that they did succeed with the results, and the experiment were published in his book, Journal of Man. In short words, Buchanan explained this phenomenon by saying that all objects have a memory since they possess a soul.'

Then, William F. Denton began his psychometry research following his inspiration from the work of Buchanan. Denton had been an American geology professor and was determined to find certain that the idea of psychometry is applicable to the geology specimens he worked with. Then, he asked his wife, Ann Denton, to aid him with his experiments during 1854. He draped a cloth across each of the geological specimens that he wanted to study. This was to ensure that Ann could not be able to see the nature of the specimens. Ann was able to take the package in her hands and placed it on her forehead. She got extremely clear mental images and with their assistance she was able to identify all the specimens accurately.

After that came Gustav Pagenstecher, who carried his research on psychometry from 1919 until 1922. He was a researcher in psychics and physician of German origin.

Between these two years, he learned the patient had psychometric abilities. The patient's name was Maria Reyes de Zierold. Maria was able to clearly talk about the history of an object as well as its present , simply by being in the presence of it, and during this she was also in a trance-like state. Furthermore, she was able to describe the experiences of the object's existence and talk about smells, sounds sights, and other emotions. Based on this knowledge, Pagenstecher developed a theory that each object contains certain vibrations that are which are condensed into them. If someone is able to tune into these vibrations, they will be able to gain insight into the experience of the object.

How Do You Know If You Possess Psychometric Abilities?

With all the discussion of psychometry sure that you are eager to find out whether you're a good psychometric reader or not. It is true that in general it's been observed that the majority of readers who read psychometrics are empaths. This is enhanced if you possess the ability to read minds to an acceptable level.

Here are some indicators:

* You feel a distinct feeling of the antique shops, which can cause you to feel odd;

You feel uncomfortable whenever there are numerous objects scattered across space, because too many objects means too much energy

* Only use brand new furniture. Furniture that is used makes you feel uncomfortable.

You are not allowed to wear jewelry or wear clothes belonging to someone else;

If you've taken a piece of used item and you are tempted in your head to wash your hands.

* You are overwhelmed going to the pawn shops.

If you've encountered any of the above indicators, then there's an excellent possibility that you'll excel in the field of psychometrics. These indicators show that an individual can discern the emotional energy of objects and explain the process that the object went through. Psychometric abilities can aid you in understanding the reasons you dislike certain objects in your home like the couch your uncle has.

3 Types of Psychometry

Object Psychometry

People are aware of psychometry and it's the most well-known of the three. As I've mentioned earlier there's some energy in every object that are made of earth. So, the person of the object who owned them leaves an unique mark of the thing.

People who are involved in object psychometry are working towards creating an excellent relationship with the object or object they're working with. They also strive to establish an intimate connection to the energies that have been imprinted on the object. There are three methods to read the imprints of any object:

* hold the object with your hands

* by placing the object on your forehead or face;

* Place the object in the solar plexus.

If you put the object either in one of the methods mentioned above or touch it, you'll gain an idea of the history of the object or who it belongs to through impressions.

Location Psychometry

This kind of psychometry is very similar to the phenomenon is commonly referred to as déjà vu. In essence, even when you've never been to an area, but you experience the sensation that you've been there and it's referred to being a form of deja vu. It is also akin to diversions of various kinds and dowsing. One example is finding out the viability for mining at a particular area by tuning to one of the samples of ore.

Some incidents leave marks in the place they occurred. This is particularly true when it comes to emotional and intense incidents. The locations are imprinted by the energy and passion of the occasion. Therefore, you are able to see the impressions.

Person Psychometry

The psychometry of this type is based on the premise that there exists an energy field that surrounds all of us. The majority of people utilize this method of psychometry. Have you ever been in an event in which you could evaluate a person's mood and mood without ever speaking to them? I'm sure you've experienced it. However there's a more frequent scenario - each encounter you have with people you've never met before, you're either disgusted by their appearance or are attracted by them. It is also due to psychological factors that affect people. There isn't a complete description of how these perceptions function, but each person can attest to their powerful effects.

How Does It Perform?

In all the explanations the researchers have given attentively to the theory of vibration that was proposed by Pagenstecher. The psyches have always maintained that the vibrations of an object are transmitted to them, and the vibrations become embedded into the object by the actions and emotions that have been accumulated over time.

Remember that the idea of communicating messages via vibrations isn't your typical New Age talk. There's a scientific basis for it too. According to "The Holographic Universe" published by Michael Talbot, the author states that the past never truly lost. However, some type of human perception is always keeping memories alive. Talbot made use of the knowledge that vibrations emanate from every form of matter that exist on Earth at a subatomic scale. With this knowledge, he concluded the notion that "reality and consciousness exist in a Hologram, where a record of the past, present, and future events is available.' It is the record which psychometrics are able to make use of to benefit.

If you look at the literal meaning behind the word "psychometry," it is essentially measuring a soul as'metry refers to measuring something and 'psych' is a reference to the soul.

The people who have the unique gift of psychometry and have mastery over the art of psychometry use their ability to see beyond objects and recognize the energy that emanates from them. It could even be defined as an energy sign. Every object attempts to communicate its own story via the energy it emits. As you are aware, the majority of people with the ability to measure psychometrics are also psychics in nature and can assist people by observing their feelings and their energy.

I've heard from many people that the most enjoyable reading experience they've experienced was with objects made of metal However, if you are able to practice enough and become proficient at the art of reading, you can be able to read every object with the same level of proficiency. For instance when one is sensitive to energy, they could even detect signals if an image of a person is displayed to them. This is the same principle of psychometric readings online, where the reader is unable to meet with the person in person.

Practicing Psychometry

Have you ever felt a negative vibes from furniture that you rent with no reason? If this happened to you, then there's an excellent chance that you'll have the ability to conduct psychometric readings since you are extremely sensitive to the energy that surrounds you.

Any strange sensations or emotions you felt are due to the energy released by objects around you. It is quite stressful for people with sensitive bodies when they are around objects shared by others or old items that are typically found in flea markets or hotels due to the fact that they contain more energy stored due to the many owners they have met in their lives. Many of these people have infected these objects with energy and whenever you come into the vicinity of them you could be spotting certain energies and energy that are conflicting.

Whatever you do you decide to do, it is important to remember that psychometry isn't scientifically proven. People use their intuition as well as other abilities to detect and comprehend the energy coming from objects. Each person's approach is unique to the one of the others.

If you'd like to try psychometry for yourself There are a few steps you must be following:

Choose a place that allows you to concentrate without distraction. Being able to think clearly is your first priority. Find a space that lets you focus on your thoughts. For instance, you could shut the shades, listen to your favorite music as well as light an candle.

* Relax; a number of famous psychics from around the world have proved the significance of relaxation during your psychometric process. They say it aids you to enter a trance and reach a higher state of consciousness. This can, in turn, assist

you in developing a stronger connection to the object you're trying to understand by using your psychometric capabilities.

You can either touch it or place the object in your hand. Then, take the object with your hands or rub it. Next you can ask someone else to put this object into your palms.

Explore your sensations, feelings, or thoughts. Then, you can begin to feel the energy the object is emitting. After that, you can sense the energy. Anything you begin feeling or thinking is a result of your senses and is typically right. At times you may be experiencing extreme emotions or seeing full-length images in your head;

* state what you're thinking. Some people think that their thought is irrelevant or insignificant and don't even say any thing. It's not a good idea since you don't have a clue as to what is important for the article you're studying.

Using Psychometry

Psychometry and cry have obvious similarities However, simultaneously there are some distinct differences too. When you try to psychometrize something, you go into the astral frequencies the object is emitting. First, you hold it in your hands and continue holding it in your hands while you are able to feel the vibrations. Then, you are able to move the object from one to another and later change it's direction within your palms. The object's awareness and the energy it emits will keep growing the more you expand the amount of contact you have with it.

Once you have reached the state of peace and complete peace, you let go of your thinking process and let your reflective abilities to begin acting. This allows your mind the freedom to experience the sensations of your body's astral vibrating. This kind of reading is completely intuitive.

After a few minutes, once you've reached a relaxed state, you'll notice an increase in flow of energy, and this growth will enable you to listen to the signals in a relaxed way. It's as if you are listening while the object talks. At last, the psychic material begins to take shape and you're in the state of "dreaming awake.' The stages continue to unfold gradually. Many people liken this psychometry process to the development of water lilies and the way they develop. The idea goes like this: the calm lake and calm water resembles your brain, and the water lilies are the tangible that is bound by psychometry. The lilies bloom from the bottom of the lake to become conscious as does your mind.

Similar to scrying, are a variety of ways the object may be presented to you. It can be thoughts, feelings or mental imagery. Whatever appears in your consciousness is something you must say out loud and speak the idea. Therefore, even if are on your own and you're practicing psychometry is a beneficial method to do it. The frequency of the vibrations is interpreted the moment your mind delved into your subconscious mind. The predictions are even more reliable when they are derived from your deep consciousness.

Your ability to predict the astral vibrations will continue growing as you continue to make advances in psychometry. As time passes, you will, too, increase your proficiency.

How do I Do Reading? Reading?

As you get used to it, it will become more easy. Psychometry is a skill that can be learned by anyone so long as you have enough compassion.

When you are taking a psychometric test here are the most basic steps you should be following:

Wash your hands thoroughly with soap and water. After that, completely dry them. This ensures that any residual energy that is in your hands has been eliminated, and it is not necessary to be hospital-sterile to do this. After the energy that was present is eliminated it won't interfere with readings.

* Now, you can create warmth with your fingertips by pressing them. This energy is generated by friction.

The second step would be to test to determine whether energy has been released or not. Start with placing the palms of your hands in such a position that they face one another. Start taking them apart. Be aware that you must break them up by about one quarter inch. Do you sense any energy or strange sensation in your palms? If so, you are experiencing energy and you're all ready to read! If not, it is a sign that you need to apply your hands more and energy will then be generated;

* Now, put the thing you wish to read with you. It is recommended to start your reading with something more of a personal nature and is a small item. For instance an item of jewelry with sentimental value is an ideal way to begin. For those who are new to the field it will be easier to move past the initial task. Another thing to bear in your mind is that

it will be beneficial when the person who's belonging that you're using isn't an individual you have a close relationship with For instance you could have a family member or acquaintances to loan the family heirloom jewelry in a couple of days.

This is likely the most crucial one - you must be relaxed! You can take whatever steps you want to achieve this goal - you may even decide to shut your eyes.

Chapter 3: What Empath People Are (The Common Personality And The Things They Fear)

A familiar personality and the things they are scared of, what they consider too overwhelming and the way their world is always able to be shifting.

If you're an empath, and you've been feeling as though you're not getting enough sleep or feeling tired towards the close of each day, or if you feel that your relationships aren't working out with people you thought were your friends Perhaps it's the right time to take a deeper examine what's taking place.

There is a possibility that you're an empath and this condition can affect individuals in various ways. Empathy is often a feeling of sadness when people are sad and being able discern the thoughts of others and feelings, which may cause some difficulty sometimes.

The energy of people around you can affect you at a deep degree because you experience their emotions and feelings like your own. Empaths are highly sensitive and often get overwhelmed by life, which makes it difficult to maintain a balanced relationship and social life.

Empaths can be mistaken with psychics due to their ability to detect the energy of others or read their thoughts. Empaths may even sense the emotions of non-animate objects like animals, plants and nature, as well as others who aren't there.

In the event that this seems to be something you believe you're having trouble with, here's an outline of the empaths' experiences with each of the signs.

Aries (Mar 21-Apr 19)

Fear: Loneliness/Rejection

They'll do anything they can to avoid feeling this way because feeling rejected or abandoned causes deep feelings of hurt and sorrow. They do not like having to be in situations where they aren't in control. They prefer to handle each situation by themselves and hope that others know how sensitive to them.

Taurus (Apr 20-May 20)

Fear: Unmet needs/being Alone

It's a stressful circumstance for them as they feel overwhelmed when their own requirements aren't being met. They are feeling like they can't perform at a high level without the acceptance and affection from others.

Gemini (May 21-June 20)

Fear: Being sloppy/manipulated

People who have a strong sense of empathy frequently encounter situations in which they feel that they are doing the same thing repeatedly and only to discover that nothing is completed. They fantasize about being able to do whatever they like whenever they feel like it.

The Cancer (June 21-July 22,)

Fear: Being Misunderstood/Burdensome situation

They may be overwhelmed by the feelings of others due to their sensitivity. causes them to feel everything in a profound way and, in some instances it may seem like a rollercoaster for them. They are typically those people who others turn to during times of need because they can make things seem easier.

Leo (July 23-Aug 22,)

Fear: Being overwhelmed by or exposed to Joy

People with this kind of empathy are often overwhelmed with joy and feel it drains a lot of them if they are experiencing excessive happiness. This is not something they can be comfortable with as they believe that pleasure should be shared with other people. In certain situations it can lead them to become judgmental of things other people do or do not have.

Virgo (Aug 23-Sep 22)

Fear: Being Judged/Rejected

Empaths are easily judged and, for the majority of the time, they want to stay away from this. They are sensitive and are able to effectively project their feelings and do not like creating emotional pain or hurt. They'll do all they can to stay out of situations in which they feel judged by their peers. They wish that people be able to see them through rather than understanding their views which tends to happen more often in the opposite direction sometimes.

Libra (Sep 23-Oct 22)

Fear: Being Alone/Lacking Control

People with this kind of empathy tend to be afraid of being on their own or feeling that the world is shifting too fast for them. They're usually seeking a partner or someone to connect with and feel in control. They don't want to be in the shadows of their environment and frequently require some space since they get overwhelmed.

Scorpio (Oct 23-Nov 21)

Fear: Being Overwhelmed/Rejection

They'll go to any lengths to stay calm And for the most part, they think that there's not enough time. They always seek some time in their busy schedules to unwind. They may become extremely emotional or angry at times and are often resented by other people due to their sensitive nature.

Sagittarius (Nov 22-Dec 21)

Fear: Being overwhelmed or ignored by everyday issues

They do not like being left out or ignored. If they feel they aren't surrounded by acquaintances or friends who truly are interested in them, they may be sad and even fail. They don't like the company of negative individuals, and tend to be overwhelmed with the thought of everyday circumstances.

Capricorn (Dec 22-Jan 19)

Fear: Feeling Used/Being Ignored

They stay clear of situations when they are feeling like they are being targeted by people who want to make them victimized. They are extremely cautious about their private lives. They try to avoid issues where they're afraid of being judged, as they would prefer to tackle issues immediately instead of let them slide into something more challenging to correct.

Aquarius (Jan 20-Feb 18)

Fear of being ignored/losing control

They feel the most relaxed when they're in charge in their own lives. They strive to create the most effective way for everyone around them to achieve what they desire. That's why they be a confident and powerful leader. They have a group of people who exude magic and usually aren't able to believe in the opinions of others or the way things ought to be accomplished.

Pisces (Feb 19-March 20)

Fear: Feeling overwhelmed or feeling alone

They don't like feeling depressed or emotionally tense due to the extent to which they can be connected to others. They aren't a fan of feeling lonely regardless of the isolated situations, and they will always find ways to complete their tasks. They are always busy and constantly have schedules, which is why they feel constantly overwhelmed by the daily things in life.

The results of your Empathy Profile Test

Like any other test of personality that you complete on the Internet it test is entirely based on how you can answer to questions from the test's creator. The test is designed to reveal what star sign or stars you connect to and in what ways. If you don't think you're connecting with your personal Empathy Profile after you take this test. If that's the case, there are other tests are available on the Internet which will accomplish exactly the same thing, and provide you a more precise reading of your own. If the test you take doesn't look like it is in alignment with your personal traits, then you should take another test until you find one that seems to be in line with your feelings and think.

The results of your Empathy Profile Test

The Dramatic Expression Profile (Emotions)

In contrast to the previous profile which just listed your personality characteristics The profile you are viewing is more detailed. It will provide you with more insight into the way you're likely to respond to various emotions. There could be some emotions that seem alike, however, others could appear different. Each person has distinct perceptions of what emotions are and what they mean to other people. The best thing you can do while taking this test is to determine how your results are related to the person you are as a person. The test creator wants to make you determine what is causing certain emotions in you and what they can mean for you. If the emotion you are experiencing doesn't appear to align with the person you are, it may indicate something else.

You'll be shown an array of emotions that are related to events that can occur in real life, and how you might react. You can click on each emotion when it appears, and it will provide additional information and questions regarding what your emotion will be. You might find that some hyperlinks appear to be similar or similar but they offer different answers. This suggests that it's possible that you're dealing with more than one emotion and you'll need to tackle each of them before they can be addressed in your life.

This could take anywhere from 10 to 30 minutes however, since it's your own initiative and you are the person performing the task, you are able to take the time you want. The more time you devote to one particular aspect the better. Anything shorter than 15 minutes is likely to be too fast. 15-30 minutes are considered normal and, in all likelihood, if have time, take advantage of even more time to your own. An extended test may give you a lot of details about you because it's more detailed than other tests administered.

These are the emotions you can anticipate to experience during this test:

Overwhelmedness: Uneasy about normal situations, and also situations where they feel that they have too much on their plate. This can be related to the work environment, relationships with loved ones, or other relationships with others.

Unsatisfied Relationships: They might think the relationships they have with others are neglected or dismissed as a matter of course and they feel dissatisfied. They might have different opinions about certain people versus othersand wish to voice their opinions particularly when they feel that people have been snatching advantage from them in some way.

The feeling that they be feeling like they are unable to get on with their lives because of the events that have occurred. They tend to be buried in the past, and are stuck on fears and anxieties that have build up over time.

Feeling unloved: They might feel that they aren't valued by others, which can lead to feelings of depression or sadness If the person they wish to spend time with does not want to see them again.

Chapter 4: Dealing With Energy Vampires

LIGHTS

For those in your life whom you have to regularly see This chapter was created to make the encounter more enjoyable. When you discover that your closest friends are energy hogs The first thought you have might be to be frightened. Take a deep breath and remember that you are able to protect yourself. You'll find a way that makes the experience more pleasant for you. The change in how you value your own experiences over those of others is now in motion. Although it may be unwise for you to choose this be aware that you experience emotions on a greater level than many. It is likely that you will be emotional as you learn how to keep yourself safe and that's fine.

It is crucial to be open about yourself and develop strategies for the people you will see frequently. These people could be your spouse as well as your children, most beloved friends, and even your friends. There are no boundaries in regards to who is an energy drainer. Your time is among many of the best resources you possess and you have the right to pick the activities you take advantage of in your day-to-day time. Be aware of how much time you are devoted to energie-suckers. Find ways to reduce this time and fill it with other activities that will inspire you and make you content.

How to handle them

Everyone is different But there are principles that can be applied to all the energy vampires that you come across. These techniques are intended to make your life more peaceful and balanced. The energy vampire is bound to attempt to drain you regardless of how you deal with it. To fight this, be sure that your spirit is kept up. Whatever it may feel however, you're in charge of this. With these strategies you'll be able to manage both your work and time which will allow you to focus for what is most important to you.

* Be aware of their existence The same way that empaths be found everywhere and so do energy vampires. They aren't going away. They will be there to contend with them throughout the rest of your life. Therefore, it is sensible in preparing yourself to face future challenges rather than believing that they will disappear. Be aware that they are attracted to the traits you possess as empath. You can provide them with what they want. If you take away the notion that you're able to stay clear of energy vampires, then you have set yourself up for the possibility of dealing effectively.

* Keep an Gut Instincts Journal The purpose of this journal is to give you an opportunity to record your feelings. Write about the people you meet each day and note the feelings they bring to you. Based on your instincts and intuition, you can make your own opinions about individuals and situations which you are not required to divulge with others. This journal will provide you with more insight to what's going on. Make sure to remain as impartial as you can about every person and event. Remember that your honesty will benefit you.

* Prioritize Yourself You're used to placing others before yourself and putting yourself first, but it's moment to change this mindset. Place your own thoughts and emotions in the center of your mind. If you'd prefer not to undertake something, do not commit to it. If you are able to imagine something that can make you feel happy, even though it doesn't benefit others, do it. You deserve to be happy without having to aid others first. This may appear to be very selfish but it's necessary

to avoid being victimized to the energy vampires that are in your life.

* Prioritize Your Alone Time The time you spend with yourself isn't selfish, it's beneficial. When you're able to have regular solo time, you'll learn how to value yourself and create a positive atmosphere for yourself. You are free to do whatever you want to do when you're at home; it's an opportunity to remind you that you are able to get to all your hobbies and interests that you have set aside to providing for others in your life.

Set Boundaries Think of ways to stop people who are energy-hungry from taking too much away from you. There is no need to be harsh or aggressive in your boundaries since it's not who you are. Find ways to convey your message without engaging in conflicts. Be aware that your feelings and thoughts are legitimate. Any person who truly values you will be able to appreciate your feelings without any questions asked.

Adjust Your Expectations: It is impossible to assume that everyone will behave like you, because not everyone is as you do. The energy vampires operate at a level quite different from the one you are operating on. They don't take into account the feelings or needs of other people before acting in the way they like. If you let go of the notion that energy vampires could become empaths you'll not be so depressed every day. You must accept them as they are based on their actions.

Don't be too generous with them If you're blessed with time and energy doesn't suggest that you must give your time and energy away. Conserving your energy and time should be a top aspect of your daily life. If you spend a lot of your time with energy-suckers do not plan your entire time around them. Set it as a matter you can handle and restrict the amount of energy you put into it. If it isn't a good feeling to you, you should find ways to end the current situation from happening.

* Beware of Your Emotions: While it is tempting to voice all of the emotions you're having to anyone that will listen, remember that energy vampires only employ this to harm you. If they are aware of how your feelings are about specific issues they could use this energy to persuade you to do something that make you feel exhausted. One example is when you are an energy vampire and they know that you are scared to drive through the freeway and they want you to pick them up at the airport since you're the only person who is concerned enough to aid them. You are in a position that you'll likely not wish to turn down. This is why securing your feelings can be helpful.

* Feel Tired: It's fine to admit that you're too exhausted to complete a task. You are only human at the end of the day. telling an energy vampire that you're too exhausted to aid them or be in contact with them isn't untruthful. It is important to watch out for your own feelings and

thoughts So letting them know that you're tired is a valid option. Don't use this as a reason to not be. It's an imperative for you to believe that you're able to take on everything life throws at you.

Know the difference between Dumping and Venting: Everyone has to vent at times But do you understand the distinction between venting and dumped? It is when someone feels overwhelmed and cannot keep their emotions in. It is likely to involve talking to someone who is able to explain the issues they're facing and are open to receiving your suggestions or suggestions. Dumping is the usual thing that people who are energy vampires do. This is when they let out all the emotions and emotions, but refusing to take your advice. So, you're left with an abundance of emotions you need to manage for yourself.

* Don't overreact. The energy vampires would like you to be able to react to what they're doing or speaking. If you can create a positive reaction, offer them the

more successful they'll be. Even though it could require some control, do not allow yourself to surrender. When you can, try not to reveal your reactions to the energy vampire's saying or doing. If they find it difficult to make a difference to you, they'll probably walk away.

Learn to say no to someone may feel like a denial to someone who is a skeptic like you, however it's a tool you need to have to defend yourself. The energy vampire might not even be able to respect you when you tell them "no," but you must learn to stick to your promise. By saying no, you are confirming that you don't want to take action. Be true to your word and be aware that you're doing it to improve your life.

* Make a reality check The life you live shouldn't be a one-way relationship where you support others. The most rewarding relationships that you can have will be ones that show the same level of respect and love. If you'd be willing to offer something to someone they aren't willing

to do in return, consider this as a way to test your assumptions. Whatever they tell you that they are in love with your character, the actions have to be in line with their words.

When you become accustomed to these techniques and techniques, you'll be able to use them to fight energy vampires. The days of feeling tired and exhausted are gone. When you implement these strategies make sure you're doing it because you realize that you are worthy of more. The energy vampires don't deserve your time, and are certainly not worth the effort. Although you can't get rid of all energy vampires that you encounter however, you'll be able to identify them with these useful suggestions. What can work for one person might not work for everyone, that's why there are so many strategies to pick from. Consider a few options and make a note of which one works best for the energy hogs that you encounter in your daily life.

If these strategies are difficult to stick to, it is because you're naturally gifted with empathy. Each one of them requires you to shift your the focus of your health. This may be a strange idea to you, since you've been devoted to other people up to now. It can take some time to become comfortable with however, it's for an important cause. When you're no longer feeling the burden of the energy vampires that hang over your shoulders, it will create a more confident and self-confident person. Instead of focusing your life on what other people expect from you, you will feel an underlying sense of pride with making every decision for yourself.

How to cut them out Completely

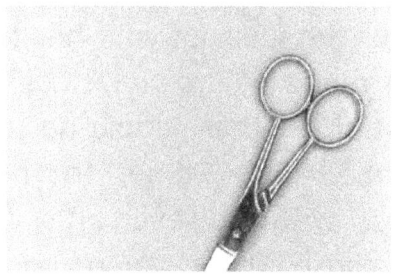

SCISSORS

In any relationship that you have within your own life regardless of how long you've been in contact with the person, you must consider the advantages and disadvantages. The relationship could be romantic or platonic, however, it could still carry the same weight when the person you're working with is a liar. You first think that you're likely to feel insecure. You've realized that are willing to let this person into your home, and they are entitled to treat you like this. It's not right. If you do invite the person to move in with you and share a bed with you, it doesn't confer on them an entitlement to treat you something other than the way they treat you. Naturally, you are able to show compassion towards others, but energy vampires don't have this characteristic. The unbalanced relationship could be the cause of a conclusion that you'd have a better life with no one living in the same space as you.

If you've thought about this, then there's nothing wrong with examining those thoughts. They're coming up due to reasons and it's clear that the person in question is impacting your mental health. Utilize the knowledge you've acquired to determine if the person really is an energy savage. Consider how you feel when you are with the person. If they were to visit in this moment do you feel anxious or happy? These small nuances are crucial in determining how they fit into your daily life. Even if they were not always an energy drainer for you, the situation can shift as you learn to get to know them better.

Many people are shocked when they discover that their love lovers are energy vampires. They could be with their partner for several years before recognizing that they are depleted of energy regularly. It can be frightening to face. It can make you consider what you've had to go through with that person. To prevent stressing yourself you should stay with the fundamentals. After you have determined the way they affect you and if they're an energy drainer then you can proceed towards the advantages and negatives. It's time to create your list which revolve around keeping them in your life , or simply walking away.

One of the cons most likely be that you regret this person. That may be the case. It's normal to feel sad about people you share a bond with, but consider how much this bond costs you and how it's effecting you. If you're close with an individual, it does not necessarily mean they are likely to improve your life. They may be in close proximity to you only for the intention of making you feel better and taking your energy. Although you may be sad for a short time, remember that this creates more space to heal and connect with somebody who is new. This is also true for platonic and romantic relationships. There is no distinction between them because energy vampires are everywhere.

Another reason to be wary of coming up is the possibility that the person will be angry with you if you say that you don't wish to have to have them within your lives. If you are someone who empathizes, this may be one of your greatest worries. While you don't want to let anyone down but there are other methods you can get your point to them. Each time you break up with an individual, it doesn't need to turn into an argument that is acrimonious. You can be sensible about it and warn them before the incident occurs. It is the first thing to express the way you are feeling. Instead of pointing fingers at them and insisting that it is your fault, just be honest to your feelings and attempt to talk to them.

The way they react to this will give you everything you should be aware of. Be prepared when the person becomes defensive or attempts to turn the entire conversation to you since this is normal for people who are energy vampires and feel threatened. If they don't react positively to how you feel, this will be their way of treating your future self too. Think about whether you want this. If you went through an extremely difficult time in your our lives, will this kind of response be enough for the eyes of a partner, friend, or family member? If no then you're aware of what you need to do.

After having this conversation, it is possible to allow the person to be alone. It's like an experiment to see what it is like to not be around them. In the days ahead be sure to not touch the person in question, no matter how often they are in your thoughts. If you have something to put down, you can write it in a journal or speak with someone who is trustworthy about the subject. In this instance, if someone reaches out to you with no prompting it will reveal something about how important the matter is to them, too. If you don't hear from them, it is a further confirmation of your initial thought regarding the person who is weighing on you.

Make contact with them again without raising any of your initial issues. You'll be able to hear what they may have to speak, but make your statement clear. State that it's your best interest to distance yourself from them for the moment. Define precisely what this means for you. For instance, if you often hung out with friends often, inform them that you don't want to do so. Be as explicit as you can for them, so that they do not have to leave with questions. When you've finished your speech and listen for any other issues come up. If not, it's time to step off. Once you're capable of doing so, consider all the benefits of the person not being within your life anymore.

It is not a matter of time, so you shouldn't think of this as something that will last forever. Instead, consider it as a moment-to-moment thing. It is the most appropriate thing for you now and you must try it. In the days that listen to the conversation you are having, be sure to keep a journal on a regular basis. This will clue you into the way you feel about this person's absence from your life. You ought to feel as if that you've got a significant burden lifted off your shoulders. If you don't have their negative influence from your life and you are able to focus on the aspects that matter most to you.

There is a feeling of guilt that can come to the surface when you have cut the person out of your life. But you can let it go. You may feel as if you've made a huge mistake , and you're worried that the person is going to alter. Be aware that energy vampires don't "change." These individuals are characterized by deep-rooted emotional issues which tend to develop into mental illness. It's not up to you to just wait for the situation to change or repair them. It is only possible to be numerous to many people and not realize this can lead you to the people who are energy hogs.

Chapter 5: The Comprehensive Guide To Psychometry

The most crucial aspect of improving your psychic abilities is to master psychometry. we'll go over every aspect of the subject in this section. In short psychometry is the technique that allows a person to instantly comprehend or "read" an object's past by touching it. They can either apply pressure to their forehead or place it in their hands. Every touch can give the user impressions of the object. These impressions could take the form of smells, sounds or images, feelings, or even taste.

What's Psychometry?

Psychometry is a unique skill that allows people to learn to perceive things that aren't accessible within the world. It is sometimes called the ability to see with a psychic perspective. Different people see in different ways. People use the surface of black glass, water or a crystal ball each has their own method. The primary characteristic in psychometry is the fact that one can develop this remarkable ability by using contact.

Someone with psychometric abilities is usually known as a psychometrist. Let me provide the way this is accomplished. Imagine you gift them a watch from the past, and they put it in their palms. They will be able to tell you everything about that watch , and the person who was the owner of it through their touching. They might also be able to talk to you about different experiences that the owner had while they owned the timepiece in their collection. You'll be amazed learn about the various things psychics can reveal to you. They may give you an insight into what the person who owned the watch was like, the things they did during their life or even when they passed away. In all items, the most significant thing the psychic is able to reveal is what that person felt at a particular point in moment in their life. There is a belief that objects are able to very effectively retain a person's feelings in it, and, consequently, even psychometrics can detect the emotions of a person very quickly.

It is important to remember that a psychometric may not have the same degree of sight/reading for all kinds of objects. The precision of their abilities varies between each object other. Many people are confused by the fundamental concept behind psychometry. It's not focused on the future , but on the present and past. This is the reason it is different from a standard read from a crystal ball.

The idea of psychometry as well as the word itself was invented by Joseph Rhodes Buchanan, an American doctor and physiologist. He explained psychometry by using an example from geologists. Similar to geologists who examine the past using fossils, psychometry can be compared to mental fossils. A thing gives the energy of a certain object and is utilized to examine the science and the development of human minds.

In essence, psychometrists hold the view that every thing on earth has a soul, which includes objects. They develop a memory by the way a person is interacted with them. It is possible to determine the past of an object or the owner of it when they are able to sense the energy that emanates from the objects.

A An Introduction to Psychometry

In the year 1842 Joseph R. Buchanan was the first person to coin the term "psychometry. The term originates of two Greek words namely psyche as well as metron. In this case, psyche is a reference to'soul and metron translates to "measurement. In all the research conducted using psychometry Buchanan is among the first people to develop it and was an American professor of physiology. He kept various types of substances inside glass bottles. Then, he asked his students to touch the vials and determine which kinds of drugs had been stored in them by the ability of touch. It was more than luck that they were successful in their quest, and the findings of this experiment were revealed in his book, Journal of Man. To summarize it in an easy phrase, Buchanan explained this phenomenon by saying that every object has the capacity to keep a memory in their minds due to their'soul.'

Following that, William F. Denton began his own research in psychometry, after being inspired by the work of Buchanan. Denton had been an American geology professor and his objective was to test whether the idea of psychometry worked with the geology specimens he uses. Then, he asked his wife, Ann Denton, to assist him during his experiments in the year 1854. He grabbed a piece of cloth and put it around the geological specimens he wanted test. This was to ensure that Ann was unable to discern what the specimens were. Ann was able to take the package in her hands and put it on her forehead. She got vivid mental images and thanks to them she was able identify all the specimens accurately.

After that came Gustav Pagenstecher, who carried his work in psychometry from 1919 until 1922. He was a psychic researcher and medical doctor with German origin. Between the two He was able to discover the patient was possessed of psychometric abilities. The patient's name was Maria Reyes de Zierold. Maria was able to talk clearly about the previous history objects and the present of it by being in the presence of it, and during this she also went into a trance state. She could describe what she experienced with the object's existence and then describe the sensations, sounds, smells and other sensations. Based on this fact, Pagenstecher come up with a theory that states that every object emits certain frequencies into it. And if an individual can detect these vibrations, they could gain insight into the experience of the object.

How Do You Know If You Are a Psychometrically Able Person?

In all the talk regarding psychometry, I'm certain you are very interested to learn whether you are a psychometric expert or not. It is true that in general it's been discovered that the majority of readers who read psychometrics are empaths. This is enhanced if you possess the ability to read minds to an acceptable level.

However, to give you more information of how to be sure that you have psychometric capabilities (or not), here's a few indicators to be looking for.

* You can feel a distinct feeling of the old-fashioned stores or they just make you feel strange.

* If you have too many objects within an area, you feel uneasy as many objects carry excessive energy.

* You should only buy new furniture. Furniture that is used makes the user feel uncomfortable.

* You are not allowed to wear jewelry or clothes of another.

If you've taken a piece of used item You have this urge to keep it in your mind to clean your hands.

You are overwhelmed when going to Pawn shops.

Are you suffering from any of the signs described above or like that? If so, you have a good possibility that you'll excel in your psychometric skills. The above indicators indicate that an individual is able to understand the energy of the object, and then describe what the object went through. Psychometric abilities could aid you in understanding the reasons you don't like some objects in your home like the couch your uncle has.

3 Types of Psychometry

Let's take a an examination of the three types of psychometry. three types of psychometry -

Object Psychometry. It is the form of psychometry that the majority of people are aware of which is also the most well-known out of the three. As I said before that there's some energy in every object that are made of earth. The person who owned the object creates a unique impression of the item.

The people who practice object psychometry are working towards creating an effective connection with the object or object they are working with. They also strive to establish an intimate connection with the energy that has been imprinted into the object. There are three ways to read the imprints of any object.

* Holding an object with your fingers

* Place the object on your forehead or face

* Place the object on your solar plexus

If you put the object in one of the ways mentioned above or touch it, you'll learn more about the past that the item has or the person who owns it by the impressions.

Location Psychometry. This kind of psychometry is quite similar to what is commonly referred to as déjà vu. In other words, even if you've never been to the location, and you experience the sensation that you've been there and it's referred to by the term "death-de-vu. It is also akin to diversions in various forms and dowsing. One example is discovering the possibility for mining at a particular area through tuning into some of the mineral samples.

There are traces left behind by the events in the place they took place. This is particularly true in the case of emotional or emotional occasions. The locations are imprinted by the intensity of the particular event. This is why you can look up the impressions.

Person Psychometry. This psychometry method is based on the notion that there exists an energy field around all of us. Most people use this method of psychometry. Have you ever had an instance where you could assess the mood of a person without having a conversation with them? I'm sure you've experienced it. There's a extremely common scenario: every when you meet people you've never met before, you're either dispelled by them or attracted by them. This is due to psychological factors that affect people. There isn't an exact explanation of how these sensations function, but all will confirm that they create a strong impact.

How Does It Perform?

Of all the theories the researchers have paid particular attention to the theory of vibration suggested by Pagenstecher. Psychologists have always believed that the vibrations of objects are transferred to them and these vibrations are embedded in the object through the action and emotion which were stored over time.

Remember that the idea of communicating messages via vibrating sounds is not typical New Age talk. There is a solid scientific foundation for this. Michael Talbot wrote a book known as THE HOLOGRAPHIC UNION and in that book the author states that the past will never be ever truly gone. In reality, some kind of human perception keeps memories alive. Talbot made use of the scientific understanding that vibrations are released by all kinds of matter that exist on earth , at a subatomic level. Based on this knowledge Talbot stated the notion that "reality and consciousness exist in a form of Hologram, where a record of the past, present and the future is present. This is this recording that psychometrics may utilize to benefit.

If you look at the literal meaning behind the word 'psychometry', it's about measuring the soul as 'metry' is a way of measuring something, and 'psych' is a reference to the soul.

People who possess the unique gift of psychometry and have learned the art of psychometry use their ability to see beyond objects and comprehend the energy coming from them. It is even defined as an energy sign. Every object attempts to communicate its own story via the energy it emits. You've probably noticed that the majority of people with psychic abilities also are empaths in nature and can help people by observing their feelings and emotions.

I've heard from a lot of people that the most enjoyable reading experience they've experienced was with objects made of metal If you've practiced enough and are proficient in the art of reading, you can read almost anything with the same skill. If someone is extremely sensitive to the electromagnetic field, they may detect signals when an image of a person is displayed to them. This is also the foundation of psychometric readings on the internet where the reader can't meet with the person in person.

Practicing Psychometry

Have you been to a second-hand retailer or antique shop and experienced an odd sensation? Did you get a negative vibe from the furniture you rent without any reason? If this is the case for you, then there's the possibility that you're able to read psychometrics since you are extremely sensitive to the vibrations around you.

The strange feelings or sensations you felt are due to the energy that's given to the environment that surround you. It can be very stressful for sensitive people to be around objects shared by others or old items that are typically found in flea markets and hotels due to the energy stored up because of the many owners they've had to deal with throughout their lives. Every single person have infused the objects with their own energy and consequently, when you come in the vicinity of them, you may be spotting an energy and aura that is conflicting.

Whatever you do you decide to do, it is important to remember that psychometry isn't supported by science. People utilize their individual strengths of intuition, as well as other abilities to detect and comprehend the energy emanating from objects. Each person's way of thinking is different from the others. For instance, some people may be detecting an emotion , while others depend on their sense of smell or vision.

If you'd like to try psychometry on your own There are a few steps that you must follow -

* Choose a location in which you are able to think freely without distraction. Being able to think clearly is your first priority. Select a setting that will help you focus on

your thoughts. For instance, you could shut the shades, listen to your favorite music or ignite an ember.

* Relax. The significance of relaxation during the psychometry process has been proven by a variety of prominent psychics from around the world. They assert that it assists you to enter a introspection and reach an even higher state of consciousness. This can, in turn, assist you in developing a stronger connection to the object you're trying to understand by using your psychometric capabilities.

You can either touch the object or place them in hands. Take the object with your hands or even touch it. Another thing you could do is to ask someone else to put it in your hand.

• Explore your sensations or feelings. Begin to feel the energy emanates from the object. Let yourself feel the energy. Anything you begin feeling or thinking is a result of your gut and is generally right. Sometimes you may be experiencing intense emotions or visualizing the whole picture in your mind.

"Speak what you're thinking. Some people think that the thought they're thinking about isn't important or significant and don't share any thing. However, you shouldn't since you never have a clue about what is important to the subject you are studying.

Using Psychometry

Psychometry and crying have obvious similarities However, simultaneously there are differences too. When you try to psychometrize the object you dive into the astral vibrations the object is emitting. It is first held in your hands and continue in the cradle while you feel the vibrations. Then, you are able to move the object from one to the next and later change it's direction within your palms. The object's perception and the energy it emits will keep growing the more you expand the amount of contact you have with it.

When you reach this state of peace and total peace, you let go of your thinking process and let your reflective abilities to begin acting. Your mind gets the freedom to experience the physical sensations that come from your body's astral vibrating. This kind of reading is completely intuitive in the natural world.

Once you're in a more calm state, you'll experience an increase in the energy. This increases your ability to take in the signals in an empathetic way. It's almost as if you're listening while the object continues talking. The material in your mind begins to forge its own path, and you are in the state of "dreaming awake. The stages continue developing in a progressive manner. It is actually commonplace to are comparing this psychometry process with the development of the water lilies and the way they develop. The idea goes like this: the calm lake and tranquil water is like your mind, while the water lilies are the physical bonds that psychometry creates. In this case, the lilies spring from the bottom of the lake and into consciousness as does your mind.

Similar to scrying, are a variety of ways the object may be presented to you. It can be ideas, thoughts or even mental images. Whatever comes to your mind You should speak it out loud and then verbalize the idea. Even if you are on your own and you're practicing psychometry this is an effective method of doing it. The frequencies are processed the moment your mind delved into your subconscious mind. The predictions are more reliable when they are derived from the deepest part of your consciousness.

Your ability to predict the astral vibrations will continue improving as you make advances in psychometry. As time passes, you too, will get better.

How do I Do What is a Reading?

Like any other talent the more you work at it the better you be at delivering readings. As you get better at it the skill will become more easy as well. Psychometry can be taught by anyone, as long as you display enough compassion.

If you're performing psychometric tests Here are the most basic steps you must follow

Step one is to wash your hands using water. After that, completely dry them. This will ensure that any residual energy that is in your hands has been removed, however you don't have to be hospital-sterile to do this. After the energy that was present is eliminated it won't interfere with the readings.

* Now, generate some warmth with your hands by pressing them. This creates energy through friction.

Chapter 6: Spiritual Hypersensitivity And Empaths

A lot of people who exhibit these traits are often described as "sensitive" people. Empaths are one of the subsets of "sensitive" people who possess an additional level of energy that affects them through their thoughts, emotions and actions in ways which other people are unable to sense or feel. This unique gift could be viewed as the negative aspect of the golden rule. We are inclined to sympathize with those who are in poverty, who are sick or are women or children in certain parts around the globe. They don't always deserve our sympathy however our compassion for them certainly does.

It is an amazing gift, one that takes time to refine and train. It's something that should be appreciated so that it becomes your best friend , not your biggest enemy. It can ruin relationships and careers within a matter of minutes. It's a gift that, is not properly trained could cause harm to the people who have it. It's a gift that is accompanied by an "scarlet letter" with it. It makes others fear them and is the reason why empaths frequently don't know how to be a part of society.

Empaths experience everything on an emotional level, often over the top. It is possible to feel the emotions of other people as if they are yours and this can affect your mental well-being and health to the point that it causes anxious attacks and panic attacks. You might have experienced this in specific situations previously. It could be that you feel like you're being exposed to harmful chemicals and you aren't able to figure out the reason. Your workplace or home could be in good shape however, you are feeling sick upon entering a specific area. It is easy to feel the feelings of other people pressing on your skin as if it were a scratchy wool sweater that will not be able to go away.

Empaths have the ability to sense and are required to master this throughout the course of their life through improving their intuition through meditation, prayer, or visualization methods.

It's depressing enough to feel as if you're continuously monitored by a mysterious force. When spiritual hypersensitivity is coupled with religion, the anxiety increases. You're not only nervous and fearful -- you believe that there is someone who is out to harm you and weaken your beliefs because of your religion.

Here are the best strategies to manage spiritual hypersensitivity:

1.) Take a look at the situation from a different perspective.

Have a family member or friend one who isn't a fan of your beliefs . They can give an impartial opinion about what's happening within your own life. This could range from their thoughts on the current situation, or how they view the overall situation in your current situation. Their perspective could be the perfect complement to the way you view it.

2.) Change One Change

Find an event that has made a difference in your life and then attempt to concentrate on it for a few minutes before making changes to everything else that is going on around you. For instance, if your loved ones pass away and makes you unhappy and angry, make an note of what has changed, and then focus on it until you feel more comfortable. Once you begin to feel better then let it go and get on with other things.

3.) Examine the Patterns

Note how a recent alteration in one aspect of your life triggers another one in another. Sometimes, these events occur quite quickly, for example, when you experience a stressful event at work, and you have a fight with your spouse at night. Sometimes it is possible that the changes don't be noticed immediately however, they could be monitored with attentive monitoring.

4.) Look for Reassurance

Although this may temporarily ease the stress but it's still vital to be reassured about the current situation in your life , especially when such changes occur. Write down everything you are aware about, and minimize the reasons you might be feelings.

5.) Define Your Values

Make time to select the items you value most to you. It could be as easy as composing the top five of your most loved hobbies or five favourite films about each subject, and then putting them in a row or as complicated as asking your family members to find a an agreement. The goal is to ensure that your beliefs being reflected by your choices, but that they're also put in the right place to influence others in your life.

Do not forget that importance of core values, too. They could be the foundation on which to tackle some most difficult issues you're facing. For instance, if angry spirits are causing you trouble and you are suffering from a recurring nightmare, they might want to make you pay for your actions of kindness towards other people.

6) Set Boundaries

If you believe about the afterlife, for instance, or the afterlife it could be beneficial to establish boundaries. It could be through ideas and thoughts about what happens following death, or even about how long you'll be able to remember someone who died before their memory is gone forever.

Chapter 7: How To Protect Yourself From Energy Vampires

E

Nervous Vampires are prone to attract empaths due to the fact that they know what they're doing. There is a chance that you have one or two energy vampires in your life if consider yourself an empath. Now is the time to recognize these individuals. If you know the signs to look for and avoiding them, you'll be able to be more secure. Be aware that empathy is a blessing. If you make the most of it you can use it as an instrument to create lasting connections with people. However, there will always be people who just want to profit from your energy, just like energy vampires. These are the people you cherish as well as strangers in the street. Everyone could be a energy hog So keep an open mind when you learn further about these people. Check out if someone you've met that is in line with the definition.

Different types of Energy Vampires

Similar to empaths, vampires can be different individuals. They aren't all identical or act similar. What they share in common may be subdued, to the point that you aren't able to recognize them initially. If you're having trouble determining the reason for someone's behavior that makes you feel uneasy it is possible to evaluate their personality. These are the most popular types of energy vampires that have been profiled. If you know someone you believe is an energetic vampire you'll likely be able classify them, or any specific traits they possess, into one of the following categories:

Victim vampire

Victim vampires are the kind of person who believes they are in the hands to the universe. They've got a long list of those who have done "wrong against themselves," and they believe that, if not for them their lives could have been much better. Everyone is plotting against them. If you approach the victim vampire They will claim that your words or actions changed their lives. They'll make you appear to be the villain.

Innocent vampire

There are many energy vampires who are criminals. There are some energy vampires who could be people you cherish. In the majority of cases they're people who have legitimate reasons for relying on you. For example, if your spouse is injured and they are forced to depend to you for help, your young brother isn't getting any less dependent or your parents are constantly looking after you. It's okay to assist those people in whatever they ask from you, but while you're at it, you must make plans to ensure they become self-sufficient as quickly as feasible.

Narcissistic vampire

Narcissists cannot demonstrate compassion. They are prone to be sneaky using a mask and a fake identity and once you let down the veil, your true character is revealed. The narcissist is only concerned with their own wants and needs. They'll do anything to make sure they've obtained what they wanted from you. A narcissist is delighted when they see an empath, because they know that empaths are easy to take advantage of. They can take away your energy due to their destructive nature. If a narcissist is able to manipulate you, they'll remove you from their life.

Dominator vampire

This type of vampire attempts to be involved in everything you do through becoming overbearing. They are determined to have an impact on your life to the smallest of details. If you let them down from any decision you take They become angry towards them. The desire to control others comes from an insecurity. They fear being perceived as weak. They are vulnerable to attack due to their sensitivity. A vampire who is dominant will overwhelm you with their presence , and an unending need to become the creator of your life. because of this they take away your energy.

Melodramatic vampire

Melodramatic vampires are excellent at creating situations. They will always get you in danger that could be easily avoided by following the basic principles of good deeds. It is possible to be enjoying yourself when they engage in an argument with a random person and put your life in danger. What's happening to the melodramatic vampire is that they are depleted in their lives. They are not living a life for, and so, creating drama becomes their primary habit. Melodramatic vampires are incredibly determined, but you must to be especially ruthless when you wish to rid of them.

Judgmental vampire

These types of vampires are prone to making judgements about everything you do. They want to make you feel guilty about your choices or actions. If, for instance, you purchase a gift for your beloved The judging vampire could make up a false story about the need to accept the love of your life. They're intent on tarnishing your image and making you appear insignificant. Empaths are sensitive. when they are judged by someone else's actions they feel slighted. Empaths should be cautious around people who are judgmental to avoid having their feelings hurt and, as a result, experiencing the drain of energy.

Blamer vampire

The vampire who is blamed cannot take their own responsibility for the things that went wrong with their lives. For example, if you help your friend submit an application to college and their application is rejected and then they blame you for making their application not get through, they're certainly the blamer vampires. A vampire who is blamed refuses to control their own life , and seeks others to blame for the things that are going on in their life. A blamer vampire can't take on tasks by themselves. They assign tasks to their victims. If they get things into the dog's mouth, they pull up the blame game, however should their plans fail -- they'll revel with glee.

A sexy vampire

The jealous vampire can never be content for anyone. The jealous vampire doesn't stop there. They'll try to harm any person they believe is doing better than they are. The person who is jealous will come up with plans to hurt someone, which leaves the person in a state of grief. If, for instance, you convince someone to become your spouse A jealous person could make contact with them, and then say lies and cause a smear on your name and making your partner think of you in a negative manner. The jealous vampire loves seeing suffering people.

Whining vampires

It's not just exhausting to be around them, but they are also annoying. When they face the slightest problem, their first response is to whine and complain about it instead of taking action. If you are with someone who is constantly whining, their negativity will eventually catch up with you and makes your energy levels decrease. People who whine can influence you into thinking negative thoughts, which hinders your ability to move forward. The empath should be aware of people who are prone to complaining and cut them out of their lives.

INSECURITY VAMPIRES

Certain people are so unsecure that they become energy hogs. The issue with being anxious is that it causes you to seek ways to compensate. If, for instance, an individual who is small is not sure regarding their size, they could have a habit of making themselves appear taller. They'll come across as trying to be a jerk, which can restrict their conversations with others. If a person is suffocating with anxiety, others tend to be suspicious of them. This can lead to people fighting in conflicts on the astral and emotional levels.

How to Identify and begin to protect yourself from Energy Vampires

Have you ever been to a place with a great feeling of energy, but after spending time in the place you felt exhausted of energy? Have you had a conversation with someone and, after having a chat with them, you felt like you were drained of energy? Both of these instances suggest a connection with the energy-hungry. Most energy vampires are attracted by their own desires are not compassionate, and are completely undeveloped.

A person who is an energy savage can make you feel exhausted stressed, frustrated and overwhelmed. It could be anyone: family members, friends, colleagues and so on. If you discover that someone you know is an energy vampire, be nice to yourself and eliminate them completely from the rest of your world. The removal of an energy vampire isn't an act of self-interest; it is a self-defense act. The energy vibrations vampires are very low.

If an energy vampire is close to you, you'll be uncomfortable, and eventually your energy levels will go through an enormous drop. Here are some of the aspects that happen when you are attacked from an energy vampire

NAUSEA: Following a meeting of an energy vampire you may experience nausea. An abdominal ache can be a sign of this. This is due to the fact that your body is under lots of stress as a result loss of energy. When you have eliminated the energy vampire, stomach pain and nausea will disappear.

A HEADACHE: An energy vampire can also cause an awful headache. When your energy levels drop lower, you'll have less energy available for your brain. The brain responds by generating an awareness that the body is depleted of sugars. The brain is a major part of an individual's energy. If the energy level drops in a person's capacity to utilize their cognitive faculties is severely affected. If you discover that you're dealing with an energy hog and you want to stop them, the best option is to remove the person off from the life of you. But, there are times when you're stuck in their presence because they play an essential roles in your daily life. Here are some tips to protect yourself from attacks from energy vampires

Set boundaries Set boundaries: Inform the person that you do not have any unchecked limits. This limits the amount of time you spend around the energy hog.

Recite positive mantras: Mantras are short sentences that people repeat to reinforce a certain conviction. Bring more positivity to yourself by repeating mantras.

Visualization: With your eyes, imagine the appearance of a light-colored membrane around the body to protect your energy from depletion. It can significantly decrease how much energy is that is lost in the direction of vampires.

Chapter 8: Tips To Manage Your Empathy Without Getting Tired

Set Healthy Limits

Being naturally compassionate and concerned for people around them, empaths struggle to say "no." This can lead to problems when you are overly committed and exhaust your energy. You must be aware of how long you listen to challenging people and learning to say no.' Set clear boundaries and limits with people, and then cut off their communication at the point when they become negative or even explicit. Rememberthat saying 'no' can be the complete sentence.

Practice Mindfulness

Empaths should set aside the time to pay attention as they can get distracted by what's happening within them. Be careful and practiced can help you reconnect with yourself. Concentrating on your breathing and perseverance, calms the mind and helps to center you within your body. It is beneficial during meditation to do "non-identification" with others. take a moment to consider yourself and your feelings as independent of any other person's.

Do not ignore your inner Critic

The inner voice that is vital to us is like a nastier coach who lives in our minds in a constant state of waiting for an opportunity to knock us down. Empaths, because they are sensitive, are vulnerable to self-critical thoughts. They could believe things such as, "Why do you feel constantly? What's wrong?" or "You're simply oversensitive." However, it's essential not to consider self-deflections, or follow your inner critic's sour advice.

Do self-compassion exercises

Although it is easy that empaths feel compassion for other people but it can be difficult to feel empathy for them. Self-compassion is the normal (yet robust) way to treat yourself as a friend. Because it's something you become better at as time passes, it's known as a method. There are three components to self-compassion practice:

1.) Accept and acknowledge your struggle.

2.) You must show kindness and compassionate in the face of suffering.

3.) Remember that imperfections are part of our human experience and is something that we all share.

Take a walk in the nature

Nature's healing effects are amazing for everyone however, it is particularly beneficial for empaths. The writer John Burroughs said, "I visit nature in order to rest and relax and also to have my senses reorganized." Since empaths are highly sensitive people (along with the environment and sounds surrounding them) being in the natural environment is the best way to recharge and relax. If your home allows you to stroll along the beach, trek through the woods, or simply sit in an open space, it's essential to recharge in a serene, natural environment, particularly when you're feeling stressed or physically exhausted.

When we are done with our day, it's essential to acknowledge the blessings that are right and empathy for the challenges. In a world in which so many people struggle to understand and express their emotions empathic thinking can appear to be the power of a superhero. Welcom to yours!

How Empaths Can Find Balance

Use these strategies to calm your mind and center yourself.

- Allow time for quiet to unwind emotionally. Make a habit of taking a few relaxing breaks during the course of your day. Get some fresh air. Stretch. Do a short walk around the office. This will reduce the over-stimulating effect of working for hours.

* Practice guerilla meditation. To combat emotional stress be quick and relax for a short time. This helps you focus your

energy to ensure that you don't absorb it from other people.

• Define and respect your empathic needs. Make sure you are protected from sensibilities. Here's how to do it.

* If someone is asking too much of you, politely inform them "no." You don't have to explain the reasons. The phrase, "No" is a complete sentence.

* If your level of comfort is three hours for socializing, regardless of how much you love peoplearound you, use your car or another alternative plan of transport to ensure you're not left in the dark.

* If crowds are overwhelming and overwhelming, you should eat a nutritious food item in advance (this will make you feel weak) and then sit in the edge of the theater, state or celebration, and not in near the in the middle.

* If you're feeling sucked by perfume, then insist that your friends refrain from wearing it around you. If you are unable to stop it, make sure you stand in front of an

open window or take regular breaks to breathe in some fresh air outside.

If you are prone to overindulge and reduce unfavorable feelings, then try the guerilla mediation mentioned above prior to being tempted to go to the fridge which could be a source of tempting temptation. In case of emergency ensure you have a cushion near the refrigerator so that you will be ready to meditate instead of a binge.

You should have a separate space within your home. You won't be overwhelmed by the feeling of excessive intimacy.

As time passes, I recommend making this list a part of your daily routine to ensure you're protected. It's not necessary to reinvent the wheel every when you're experiencing emotional stress. Utilizing practical methods to deal with it empaths will have faster reactions, feel more confident and their skills can grow.

Chapter 9: What Is It Mean To Be An Empath?

Empaths aren't something you can escape from. If you're an empath then every aspect of your life will be affected. It is impossible to enjoy the benefits of being an empath , and get rid of the negative ones. When being an empath provides people the capability to understand about the emotions and feelings of loved ones, then you must also be open to being bombarded with emotions and feelings of people you meet on the road and in your work place. This isn't a choice.

Empaths have profound effects on every aspect of life. From your health, to your relationships and work being an empath impacts every aspect of your life. It's impossible to live the same life as regular people. You'll face unique challenges and opportunities you'll have to master to manage.

Health

The health of an empath suffers the most severe impact. It is possible to be an empath of any kind. Your ability to empath can help you achieve your goals as well as your intuition, psychic skills, or anything other than that. You can clearly see that a lot of these abilities are associated with your brain. However, this doesn't mean they won't influence your physical, mental or mental health.

Being empathic makes you an open-minded person. Empaths awakened have more distinct personal boundaries. As a result they are less influenced by the energies that surround their bodies. Empaths who are not awake are less secure and are affected more. Yet, they are all still affected. The only difference is that empaths that are awake have more clear personal boundaries. This means that they are able to handle the influences better and have a better chance in facing the challenges.

Even empaths who are awakened can't stop the absorption of emotions or emotions and energy. However, they're better at discerning the emotions and emotions that are theirs and the ones that aren't. However those who aren't awakeed empaths find it difficult to handle the constant influx of feelings and emotions since they cannot distinguish between their own from others.

Also, it has major influence on the empath's daily life as well as their interactions with others. No matter what level of consciousness, getting outside is a challenge. It is inevitable to be inundated by a plethora of emotions and sensations when you are in crowds. This can make you feel tired and exhausted. It's an occupational risk that comes when you are an empath. It will be helpful to be able to handle it correctly.

environments that have a lot of sensory stimulation don't work well with empaths. For instance, empaths isn't likely to find dance bars with loud music appealing. There is too much physical and loudness. They may become over-stimulated. Being an empath you should be aware of the areas that are feasible.

Contact with physical objects of any kind should be avoided by all types of empaths. That doesn't mean that you shouldn't touch other people or hug your loved family members. It's just that shaking hands with people who you do not know isn't a good matter for you. It's probably a standard for some and a socially acceptable salutation, but it could be draining for someone who empathizes. Although it is possible to feel happy by shaking hands or embracing someone you admire and love however, shaking hands or embracing someone you've never met could drain your energy. Making alternative ways of greeting people will help you to develop empaths. You can greet people by folding their hands, as is the norm in Eastern cultures, or bow a bit.

If you're an emotional empath it is normal to be affected deeply because your body is more open to emotions, feelings and energy. You'll need to be more adept at discerning between different emotions that are infiltrated. As an emotional empath it's impossible to avoid the absorption of energy; However, if it's possible to improve your interactions with people who have positive vibes and positive vibes, you will gain from these. As an empath you'll still absorb energy. It should be positivity energy that is in same amounts you receive as it makes healing easier.

Being a physical empath won't be able to be any less difficult. A physical empath is able to sense the physical suffering and pain of others who are around them. This means that if you're near someone who has skin rashes, then you can be sure to suffer from them. This requires extra care. However, there's some benefits to this. If you interact with healthy people with positive energy, you could even be a part of that energy and grow from it. It's a powerful power.

While it's simpler to recommend mixing with a small number of individuals, we are aware that it's not feasible for all purposes and in all circumstances. We'll meet all kinds of people and be able to exercise a limited control. Thus, it's helpful to remain more attentive about your mental health.

Anxiety, low energy levels or sadness, as well as mild stress are a few of the more common symptoms that indicate an impact on your well-being. If you're constantly experiencing negative emotions or uncomfortable atmosphere, you could experience these signs without any significant or obvious cause. This should be an indication that you are required to take immediate action within your business or expand your boundaries.

If you don't take note of these issues the signs, they could cause extreme anxiety, depression and even rage.

In too long the midst of a chaotic environment is not advised for empaths since it could be extremely imposing on the character that the empath.

Maintaining a high level of one's physical, mental and emotional levels is essential for empaths since they will carry more burdens at the at the end of the day. If they start the day with a lot pressure, this could significantly hinder their ability to perform.

Since being an empath isn't an illness, there's no cure for it. But, there are methods to increase your personal boundaries and keep the invading emotions from impacting your mental and emotional well-being.

A balanced diet that includes plenty of fruits and vegetables will give you the strength and energy to get rid from the typical stress. Also, you should meditate regularly as it will help in calming your mind and your heart even under the most stressful situations.

If you feel overwhelmed by your emotions and don't want to carry any additional burden You must take a break and retreat to a peaceful place, or the peace of nature until your healing is completely.

Empaths need to deal with their health concerns generally, and quickly.

Neglecting these issues could have a an impact over the long term on mental, physical and emotional health. the process of recovery can be slow and difficult, if it is any at all feasible.

Love, relationships and sexual life

These are the most important issues of life, and empaths can be a struggle in any instances if they fail to manage them properly. We all want real friendship and love in our lives. They can help us grow as individuals. But, we all know the consequences of fake relationship and toxic ones. Even someone who is emotionally stable will find it difficult to leave an abusive relationship. The more damaging it is, the more difficult it is to break away from them. It could be a difficult task for an empath , who is bound to be more appealing for those who are dependent on them or require them. They are naturally inclined to be a hero and this could be detrimental to them.

Because of the importance of each aspect We'll go over them in order.

Love The magic of love is the potentia that heals the wounded heart for an empath. Empaths are always searching for love, even when it's becoming overwhelmed by pain and sorrow, hate and other similar deep emotions of the people around. The presence of loved ones can assist an empath to reenergize and recover. Empaths will feel more at ease in the company of one who they are comfortable with and is completely trusting.

While the heart of an empath will always in search of the company of the person he/she is in love with however, too much intimacy may turn into a tad too much. They want to be loved however, they also desire some time for themselves. The people who love you aren't focused on you, and can are able to invade your space in a way that is not conscious which can result in serious trouble.

While it's not an issue for an empath who is awakened and recognizes the need and talks about it with loved ones, those who aren't awakened empaths tend to get caught up in the confusion. They're not even aware of the need, which could lead to confusion as well as mistrust and the loss of affection.

It is imperative that an empath comprehends the particular situation he or she is in and talks about it with family members before any disagreements arise. Being clear, honest and yet sensitive is the only way to reach a compromise. While this is an ideal approach, the majority of empaths be unable to find it.

Empaths can also be that they are emotionally occupied most of the time, which means they may not be capable of contributing much. It could cause someone else to feel a bit odd. But empaths need to convey this information to their family members and explain how things are going in their lives. If they can realize, love will flourish effortlessly. The problem lies in the degree of communication and understanding. The majority of empaths are able to comprehend the needs and emotions of other people without the use of words. They are able to remain in the belief that other people can be the same, and therefore they do not utilize words to convey their feelings in a way that is appropriate. This is the cause of most of the miscommunications.

Relationships: No one throws out open the doors to those who behave as empaths. It is their nature to be drawn towards those who need unconditional love and support. Narcissists are flawed people who tend to take over all the positive energy of the person who is trying to help them. The empaths might even feel this. Yet, they'll struggle to stay away from selfish or narcissistic individuals. Narcissists are motivated by an underlying sense of purpose because they understand that they're required often.

This is why empaths with an innate, shrewd self are impulsively drawn to the narcissists as well as unhealthy relationships. The relationships that are abusive quickly become violent, and empaths are aware that they are being exploited. But, they aren't capable of resisting the lure of a new attempt.

Empaths have a deep desire to assist those who are suffering, but they must realize that there's some limitation to the things they are able to accomplish. They can't continue to suffer from the wrath of their tyrants and keep returning.

They can serve as an ingredient for empaths. A good connection with a kindhearted person will help empaths live their lives effortlessly and confidently. However the narcissist will constantly make them feel inadequate and insignificant. They'd continue to be hurt inside and out and never have the time to heal their heart.

Empaths must be aware of how important relationships are in the lives of their clients as well as the roles they play. They'll have to be cautious when building relationships, and they should not forget the essential aspects of finding the right people for relationships.

Sex is something that isn't talked about much. But, not addressing sex could be a major error. The empaths view sex differently as compared to normal people. For empaths, sexual intimacy is a means to let go of the stress they carry and is not just a means to show their love to their spouse.

It is also where the fracture begins.

While the majority of people desire sexual intimacy to be an attractive expression of affection, the way empaths engage in sex and enjoy the practice, it appears like they are taking advantage of the sexual experience to get pleasure from physical touch. They are leaning more towards the side of love and more on the psychological aspect of it.

The majority of the time, their partners in love aren't capable of recognizing the difference, and start to feel like they are an person who is a source of sexual satisfaction. The common reaction is to rob empaths of sexual pleasure, and this could result in frustration or emotional outbursts and further divisions.

There are many things that aren't like they seem to those who are empaths' companions. Empaths will typically not have a sexual connection with someone who he or she does not like. It is important to understand that love is the primary reason of the sexual activity. But, empaths might not be able to convey this accurately when they engage in sexual activities.

It is the duty of the empaths , to explain their desire for sexual freedom and the importance it holds to them. After that their partner might not be able offer them similar sexual pleasure however, so long as there's an appropriate communication, everything will run smoothly.

Work

The work place is the third important aspect an empath has to face in daily life. Places that are crowded or filled with agitated people could be difficult for empaths. However, this shouldn't be an option for empaths who work in environments that are highly competitive. If an empath is required to work in places that are full of rush, excitement, anxiety, or emotions that are exuberant through the atmosphere, they will end being soaked in the emotions of a large number of people. They then store their emotions in the form anxiety, stress and fear.

This can impact the performance of employees to a large degree, as well as their behaviour at work.

Avoiding crowded or noisy workplaces isn't always possible for empaths. However, they are able to remain in a certain distance.

Empaths should realize that they aren't able to absorb energy and emotions, and be at their peak. They'll have to make appropriate adjustments.

It is better to avoid heated discussions in the workplace and have as much solitude as you can. The longer you be at your desk by yourself the simpler it will be to get out of the chaos.

It is also possible to keep plants and natural objects at your workstation to aid in transmitting feelings and energy.

Meditation regularly can serve a vital function in keeping you calm and calm even when you're in stressful environments for a prolonged period of time. If you regularly practice meditation you'll have the ability to establish boundaries for yourself and be able to distinguish between feelings and emotions which are yours and ones you've picked up from the environment.

Addictions

So far, we've discussed important issues to lead a successful life of empaths. We have been discussing the most important aspects of life that affect empaths the most.

Unfortunately, empaths of all kinds aren't able to conquer all difficulties. They have a weak energy control system. not as effective, and they don't achieve the relaxation they require. These empaths can also fall in relationships and be victimized by dominators and narcissists. energy vampires.

They find a quick escape from addiction. Gambling, alcohol, drug and sexual activity is the most common method to reduce the pain and achieve peace.

It's a way on which people can find the peace and freedom they've sought all their lives.

They wish for the constant assault of feelings to cease and it won't be able to occur until they're drunk. It is initially a reason but quickly turns into an addiction they be unable to quit.

The substances consumed can aid to intoxicate the mind as well as the sensation of numbness, but they do not solve the issues that cause them. The relief can be temporary and is a false. The temptation to give in to addictions is similar to trying to find light in the middle of the tunnel.

Drugs, alcohol and gambling are the types of media that typically receive the worst media. But, they're certainly not all addictions.

Many empaths find comfort in food, and eventually become hooked on food. They don't eat food for the sake of filling their stomachs but rather to ease their pain and distract their minds from their issues. Comfort food, high sugar desserts, and other sweets get their attention because their the high sugar content triggers serotonin release within the brain, which creates a feeling of satisfaction.

Empaths may seek satisfaction and happiness by shopping. So long as they stay completely absorbed in their shopping, they are able to distract their attention from immediate problems. We all know that this strategy does not work over the long run.

The sensation of comfort or joy cannot be achieved without an understanding of these addictions. They are only temporary distractions.

However, these addictions could cause a flood of sorrowful existence, intense anxiety and depression.

Finding a way to get rid of these addictions is the same as self-medicating in the midst of an incurable illness. The drug will not only result in more suffering and pain as well as you'll live forever in constant the fear that something awful could happen when you're done.

The best option is to seek assistance. The best method to get help for empaths is to speak to someone you trust or seek professional advice. There is no reason not to seek help since empaths, in their own way, you are a hugely talented person however it is a possibility of going down the drain because of inadequate management.

Addiction is damaging in its own way and is harmful to everyone generally. The process of getting rid of addictions is particularly difficult for empaths due their tendency to be impulsive.

If they are able to engage in more effective methods to channel their energy via exercises and meditation, they will see more positive outcomes. Meditation is an excellent method to refocus your mind and your life. It aids in grounding, and it will help you improve your mental health.

Removing yourself from unhealthy addictions is a top priority for any empath , as it can make you fall further into the deepest pit which recovery may be nearly impossible.

Chapter 10: Tips For Endurance For Empaths , Highly Sensitive And Highly Sensitive People

If you're an empath or very sensitive it could appear that your personal reality is constantly shattered by the sensations and energy of those around you. This could wear you out and force you to surrender your personal power when you're not vigilant this is the reason why it is vital to utilize all of the methods for managing stress that are discussed below.

Your generous nature and your highly flexible faculties are blessings for the world, but when they are not properly analyzed the possibility of losing them is high. If you are an empath, I would like you to keep this list handy in the event that external forces are affecting your own inner universe.

1. Be aware of the drains and Energizers

The first and most crucial thing empaths can do is identify when and when your energy levels decrease and, in turn, the aspects that demonstrate the ability to boost your energy.

By using this knowledge you'll be able to stay clear of situations that can be a problem, such as putting, or people who drain your energy. Ensure that you are spending enough time doing things that will recharge your batteries.

It could sound straightforward it sounds, but stopping the flow out and increasing the flow into are essential that allow empaths endure but also to prosper.

2. Make A Shield

There are bound to be a handful of circumstances that you as a sensitive person would like to stay away from, but aren't due to their impact on your life. Large work capacity, massive gatherings of family members, as well as other gatherings may all have people who are difficult to handle.

Because they are to a certain extent essential, you must to find out how to adapt to these conditions. Using the use of a shield for energy is one way to accomplish this.

It's going to take effort and training on your part however, eventually you can create a mental line that allows for what you would like to let into your life, but redirects any negative from your life. Simply imagine an air pocket that encompasses the entirety of your body - an space pocket filled with light. This is an excellent method of looking at the larger view. In this air pocket lies your world, where you are able to focus on your innermost thoughts and find your equilibrium as everything else are outside.

If you feel your energy is diminished by the actions of others or by an situation, you can retreat from your pocket of air and end the flow. Everything boils down to yourself and the inner you.

3. Keep Your Eyes On Your Thoughts

If you are thinking it's difficult to construct a barrier to stop negative thoughts and emotions from invading your brain, the ideal thing to do is monitor your brain to find the source.

If, for instance, you find yourself pondering angry concerns, you should determine the cause of the problem or something you've taken in from an other. When you've figured out the person who feels it and the source You can begin an exchange with your partner for a solution.

Find out what the displeasure is trying to tell you. Perhaps you feel there is something missing in your present or maybe you've found an act of another person's that is unacceptably.

Conduct a quick interview and discussion to determine if there's something that could be done to express your displeasure and then follow up with it.

ID is crucial here finding out what that the musing wants to inform you of and where it originated is a sure-fire way to either assert it and disperse the information.

4. Replay Positive Affirmations

Empaths are generally friendly and generous but it's not the norm that they are always positive. Because you are a victim of what surrounds yourself, you could feel the negative effects of sadness and apathy that's not yours. To keep your mind focused it is beneficial to have a variety of positive positive affirmations to help you overcome the conflict and return towards the sun.

5. Establishing

It could be yourself to have stronger relationship with the Earth than a lot of people, and you could use this potential advantage in the event you are aware of how.

It is possible, through the right training, to absorb any negative energy or feelings that you are experiencing and release them into the Earth to be absorbed. In essence, the connection can inspire you and out into the middle of your body.

All it boils down to isolating and strengthening the connection between yourself and Earth.

6. Pardon

Certifiable pardoning refers to the way through which the negative energy, which was repressed inside is released and swept in its direction.

No matter if it's an individual incident or something else that took place some time back in the event that you keep your hands on the wound and hold it in your hands, it will continue draining you of your power. Only when you remove yourself from the pain, will you be able start the healing process.

Being a sensitive soul most likely, you'll end in danger of being used and hurt more than the majority of people - it's due to your sensitive and generous nature. being aware of when and when to forgive is crucial for you.

Additionally, be sure to pardon yourself for anything you might have done as well as for allowing yourself to be hurt by other people.

7. Therapy

Empaths are often occupied people who are trying to deal with the multitude of emotions which constantly assault them. It's the case that you are overwhelmed by your thoughts that you forget to count and clean the emotions you experience; rather, they build up and keep in impacting your.

Therapy is when you allow you feel the emotions in their most intense crying when you feel sad or happy and shouting in anger. These are all expressions of feelings, but they can be a lot more. They can be the source of suppressed energy, no matter whether it is positive or negative.

Don't be afraid to show your emotions however short, to test and overcome them.

8. Timetable Some "You Time'

The majority of ideas in this guide are best mastered on their own that is why it is crucial to give yourself plenty of the chance to practice what you've learned.

Do not feel guilty even if you have to deprive othersyour happiness; it is essential and your family members will benefit the most out of you on possibility that they initially let you be completely independent of any other person.

If you are able to set aside two nights a week, or an hour before going to bed every night, make sure you spend the time to yourself into your diary.

9. Create a welcoming and safe Space

Simply tied to the previous idea of being unconnected to any other person, you'll really want to recoup your energy and regain your equilibrium much faster when you find a comfortable location to let loose.

Much more than other people it is a benefit to have an area that is solely to be used for unwinding. It doesn't matter if it's in the bathroom, room or some other place, you shouldn't be glued to the television, organize your day, or take calls in it - at any time. Create a space to get help specifically.

10. Eat well

This may sound strange but people who are extremely adjusted are definitely more in touch to the foods and nourishment they consume. If you eat it feels like the sensation of poo.

To avoid this ensure that you try to stick to a diet schedule that is well-balanced and well-adjusted. If you eat the right mix of fresh products from the soil and meats, beats, as well as a few little sweets (with some caution) You will be able to replenish your energy levels efficiently.

11. Yoga and reflection

Maintaining the body and psyche flexible and graceful can provide empaths with the additional capabilities they require to discover their surroundings. The benefits of practices like yoga, contemplation and other similar practices can be questioned and isn't more evident than for empaths.

12. Get Out Into Nature

The link between the empath and the Earth is well-known and the subject of discussion for a long time, so it shouldn't be a shock to find out the fact that being open to the natural world in all of its beauty is a fantastic healer for them.

Nature is filled with energetic energy. By soaking you in this for only a short moment, you will soak up this energy and revitalize your body.

13. Change your perspective on people and Energy

Being a highly sensitive individual you may at times the time be difficult to be around other people and observe them. You're on the top in terms of mindful and consideration. If you observe people engaging in reckless or a bad behavior could cause you to be upset in a significant way.

So, it is suggested that you try to erase your mind from the situation and observe these other thoughts not as insidious or terrifying instead, as uninformed or causing harm.

The majority of people who behave at the outer in the middle of the spectrum to you are acting because of their childhood or an accident they suffered some time in the past. They will not be able to see the world in the same way you imagine it and consequently do not treat it, or the people in it, as you would.

Through changing your perception of these people and their lives You can lessen the impact they have on you by unequivocal agreement. You might even discover that you are able to feel affection and empathy for these people where previously you experienced confusion and dismay.

14. Cleanse Your Chakras

Your chakras are your mystical and fiery centers within your body. Keeping them free from damaging optimism is crucial.

An effective and common method to achieve this is to use a fragrance in the treatment, and then smear. The power of aroma has been used for centuries and scents, like ones from savvy and lavender can help cleanse your chakras of any obstruction that could hinder them from performing to their full potential.

There are those who believe that certain precious stones can be used to absorb negative energy the environment and inside you.

15. Thank You For Your Gifts

The ability to be an empath, or a sensitive person may at times seem like a burden however it's an amazing gift. It is possible to experience the excitement and zing of life on a massive level , and one that other people will fight to attain.

Simply by showing gratitude for your capabilities and abilities, you can contribute to the cycle of renewal. The act of giving thanks is positive energy that will remove the negative energy and make you feel calm.

16. Place Stopping points in place

Sometimes there are people that you encounter in your daily life that, without even realizing it, enter your energy zone, that air pocket you were in prior to the chapter. This is why it is crucial to establish stopping points whenever and where you need them.

These limitations could be physical, conversational or transient. They can be various things depending on the manner in which a person uses their energy.

Keep to these cutoff points , and do not allow your mind to allow you to be a gatekeeper in the dark.

17. Assume the risk of liability

If you think that the world must be able to accommodate your precarious methods, you'll be terribly disappointed to learn that it will never happen.

In the end It is empaths who have to take some responsibility for their own success and the tips from the past can help you do this.

You must recognize that your peace of mind and euphoria come from your own efforts; although you may experience like nobody other person, you are competent to manage it. Have faith, be empowered, in yourself, and work. There is no way to be easy with a kind heart, but it is possible to achieve everything.

Chapter 11: How To Make Use Of Essential Oils And Aromatherapy To Help Highly Sensitive People

Aromatherapy can help in a myriad of ways including sleeping better and the high pressure of blood. Aromatherapy and essential oils for those who are prone to stress can be a successful method to reduce stress levels. This article will examine the advantages of aromatherapy, the way the process works and which kinds are suitable for vulnerable people.

The use of aromatic plants has been utilized to treat ailments since the beginning of time and there are records from in the third century BC in describing their healing capabilities. Nowadays, aromatic plants can be available in grocery stores and health facilities like cancer treatment centers and hospitals which help patients who are going through tough circumstances to heal quicker than they normally would. In these settings the use of aromatics is to treat more than just health reasons.

Aromatherapy is a natural method to utilize essential oils' aroma to aid in aromatherapy. The thing that makes it unique it that unlike many other types of therapy, it's completely natural and does not cause any side negative effects, as do most medicines that treat anxiety and depression. This makes it perfect for people suffering from allergies to perfumes as well as other medical conditions which prevent them from taking traditional medications.

Essential oils are extremely concentrated extracts of plants since they are rich in plants' healing properties. When you buy soaps and candles that are scented the scent is derived from synthetic fragrances, which can be dangerous in the long term. Essential oils are derived from the same place but they aren't harmful, and therefore safe to utilize.

In the past, aromatherapy has been utilized by those who have been through difficult circumstances to ease their feelings of depression. Modern medical professionals and experts have found the reasons aromatherapy can be effective. When someone who is compassionate utilizes an essential oil the aroma is released through their noses, where it triggers the release of endorphins and other hormones that feel good that ease anxiety and stress. This makes essential oils perfect for people who suffer from anxiety or similar disorders that people who are susceptible suffer from.

Essential oils are extracted from many plants. The most well-known oils are lavender jasmine, peppermint, and lavender. Lavender is among the most sought-after essential oils. It typically comes in a blend with other oils , such as lemon or Chamomile. Lavender is often utilized for sleep aids and can also boost performance all day long. Mint can also be an ideal aromatherapy oil because it contains numbing properties which ease pain and enhance the ability to concentrate. The essential oils of Mint are typically combined with orange, and emits a pleasant aroma that can ease anxiety in a matter of minutes.

The possession of essential oils at the house is essential for those who are susceptible. People who are susceptible to allergies can develop to essential oils that are common when they are used in their natural form. However mixing them together is safe due to the effects of all the aromatherapy oil that are used in a single session. It is essential to clean the airtight containers in which the essential oils are kept regularly to ensure that no contaminants are in the jar and there aren't any health risk for your family members when you make use of the oils.

Find beauty aisles at the local health store, where products without scent are available and purchase everything that you require, including lotions, creams and shampoos with no fragrance. Aromatherapy oils are also proven to be beneficial in preventing hair loss. Those who have sensitive scalps are more likely losing hair. Aromatherapy to relieve stress can be a fantastic method to ease anxiety and establish positive habits that can make your life more enjoyable.

Anna Campbell, from different essential oils of Aromatherapy For the Very Sensitive.

Chapter 12: Telepathy

Telepathy originates originated from it's Greek term "TELE" which loosely refers in "distant," and "PATHOS" or "PATHEIA" which is "feeling" also known as "perception." Telepathy can be described as "the supposed transfer of information between two people without the use of human physical or sensory channels." If we attempt to comprehend this concept in simpler terms. In this case we can define telepathy as the ability to communicate with another person without communicating or being in the proximity of the concerned person. The result will be a successful communication and exchange that is not supported by any known method of communication or contact. It will then be only based on the abilities of the mind. Because there isn't any compelling evidence to support the claim the existence of telepathy It can be regarded as a pseudoscience, in the terminology that is used by the scientists.

The history of Telepathy

It is possible to trace the beginnings of telepathy as an art form to the latter part of the 19th century, as far as Western civilisation is involved, if we go by the assertions of historians such as Roger Luckhurst and Janet Oppenheim. It was at the same time period that there was a Society for Psychical Research was established. In this period there were a number of important advancements in the physical sciences. As consequence science-based concepts began being applied to the realm of psychic phenomenon. Scientists were hopeful that this could help to develop some understanding of paranormal phenomena could be better understood of. In this situation, the concept of Telepathy, which we currently are aware of, was born.

There were certain magicians and mentalists in the 19th century. One of them was Washington Irving Bishop, who performed acts of reading that relied on only bodily signals, which he believed was because of being a muscle sensitive. Stuart Cumberland, another famous thought reader, was well-known for his blindfolded tricks. He claimed to not have psychic powers and was credited with his successes, he was able to do it with the aid of muscles sensitivity. They were in massive disagreement in their Society of Psychical Research as they were denying psychic abilities as well as marketing muscle sensitivity.

Parapsychology is a field that deals with paranormal phenomena Telepathy, which is often associated with clairvoyance and precognition, is defined through extrasensory perceptions that we may also refer to as ESP also known as "anomalous cognitive." Parapsychologists typically think that this type of communication occurs in telepathy as well as other types of unique transmissions are carried out via hypothetical psychic mechanisms, also known as "psi." The parapsychologists typically utilize certain methods to test the telepathic abilities of a person with the help of Zener cards as well as the Ganzfeld test.

From its inception until today it has been proposed several types of telepathy specifically, latent telepathy Retrocognitive, Precognitive and intuitive Telepathy, Emotive telepathy and Superconscious Telepathy. There are other types of telepathy that are also present, for instance, Dream Telepathy and Twin Telepathy. Latent telepathy which may be called deferred telepathy is the case when there is a transmission of information that has a delay that is a set duration of time between transmission and reception. In the event of a telepathic exchange between two sources regarding information from the past, the future, or even the current state, it's known as Retrocognitive, Precognitive and intuitive Telepathy. Telepathy that is characterized by emotion is also described as an remote influence or emotional transfer that transmits kinesthetic experiences via altered states. What we mean by superconscious telepathy is that it is an application of the supposed superconscious within an individual to gain insight into the knowledge of the whole human species to gain knowledge.

It's fascinating to realize that telepathy doesn't belong to humans alone. It is also known as "animal "telepathy," where there is a predisposition of thought to think biologically, in animal species. For instance, we've seen a variety of controlled and synchronized behavior among birds when they turn together. There is an instantaneous conclusion from every bird in the group when they are turning at the same time. This could be thought to be like the phenomena we are familiar with about psychic telepathy. This idea was explored by scientist Jure Demsar as well as a computer scientist in 2017 and their research led to the realization that there is to be a certain logic built in for this universal behavior of birds. It isn't necessarily in violation of the laws nature is able to create, but this behavior is likely to be part of a system of computational rules that confirms the existence of telepathy in animals.

The whole concept of telepathy is a well-known genre of fiction, whether in science fiction or modern fiction, in which characters are created to possess the ability to communicate, and add crucial tangents in the story.

What is the Science Behind Telepathy

The scientific basis for the whole concept of telepathy could be explained through ESP that is known as extrasensory perceptions. Extrasensory perception is a term that refers to the perceptions beyond the sense organs humans have, such as psychic clairvoyance, as well as knowledge of future events as well as Telepathy. A lot of people hold the opinion that because these phenomena aren't visible or measured in a way that is comparable however, they may not be real, and don't have any basis. However, recent research has been studying these subjects for a long time and has identified potential biological explanations that could be the reason for this phenomenon.

* Mirror Neurons - The science of telepathy focuses on methods of communication that do not involve the sensory organs. Certain studies have proven that it is possible to read the mind of the person you are talking to or know what they're going on in their minds at the moment due to the presence of specific neurons in our brains that act like automatic mirrors that help us understand the motives and emotions of the person in question. Gregor Domes, a psychology professor back in 2007 had discovered that this process is improved by oxytocin. It is nothing more than a form of hormone that enhances our confidence and social behaviour.

* Long-Distance Communications - Here we are referring to an idea that allows us to travel some time ahead of the year 2014, for instance. A psychiatrist named Charles Grau conducted a study in which he attempted to further justify telepathy

through his research. He proved that brain-to-brain communication is possible with the internet. The research he conducted proved that it is possible for information to be transferred across long distances when we view the internet as the road connecting the two individuals.

* Invisible Communication The year 2005 was the time Rupert Sheldrake, a biologist, decided to study the field more thoroughly. Together with his colleague Pam Smart, they hired more than 50 volunteers to take part in the purpose of a survey. They also employed four emailers. They also arranged for a set time for each volunteer and made them guess the emailer that according to their estimates, will be sending them at that time. If the percentage of correct guesses been lower the results may have been explained by simple chance or coincidence. However, the proportion that was correct for the answers was nearly 43 percent, which is too large to be explained with luck or in the context of randomness.

Additional research has already been carried out in this area for quite a while to determine the mechanism that causes Telepathy. A telepathic mentalist claimed to be telepathic was taken as a participant for a psychiatrist Ganesan Venkatasubramanian along with a few colleagues who were conducting research on brain imaging and a second volunteer was also taken to be a controlled participant. It was discovered after the study that the subject who was a psychotherapist could recreate the image that was previously created for him with great accuracy and accuracy, in contrast to the controlled subject, who could not discern the image in any way. The subsequent research into the causes of this revealed that when the mentalist was in the process of working in the right hemisphere of the parahippocampal gyrus which is also known as the PHG is highly active in him, however it wasn't the case for the subject who was controlled. Contrary to the mentalist, in the subject under control the left frontal gyrus was activated.

The results of these studies as well as historical research data suggest that our brains possess the ability to swiftly absorb subtle social signals and signs which are not necessarily transmitted through traditional methods. Additionally, our brains are able to detect automatically certain intentions and feelings when others are also present. We all know about the system of communication using frequencies that the internet utilizes. There must be something that is very similar to our brains to exchange information or have a successful exchange without using the obvious methods. The brain's neurons must be tuned to similar frequencies which allows us to communicate effectively that we can communicate, without sensory organs. If we take Telepathy as a proven fact. If so it would also be evident that certain people are more adept at being telepathic than others because of the frequency system mentioned above in which some individuals will have the frequency just right, while others will not. If we are talking biologically, it is likely to involve the hippocampal as well as the parahippocampal regions in our brains that are connected to telepathic communications. It is because it's these two regions that play a role in integrating memories as well as with specific aspects of communicating. Telepathy, in turn, is a result of getting to know the person you are talking to. The more familiar you are with the person you would like to talk and the more easy it will be to transfer thoughts and feelings. In essence, the frequency is higher if both the sender and receiver are familiar with each other.

The Signs You Have Telepathy abilities

In the beginning, it's important to recognize that there is a vast distinction in the two terms "psychic" abilities and "telepathic" abilities. They're not alike and therefore, should not be misunderstood. Let's try to discover how one can determine whether they have powers of telepathy at all. What are the ways that one is able to recognize their own abilities? It is possible that it will be that we accept things on their merits believing that they are chance or coincidence, however, the truth is far more complex than that and it is connected to telepathic channels.

* Telepathy and Intuition . All of us at one time or another has felt the phenomenon of intuition, which is nothing more than getting an impression in your body that triggers a sort of premonition of what is about to occur, and then you get an notion of the outcome of it prior to everyone other people. Sometimes we dismiss the feeling as a simple chance, but the reality does not happen that way. This could be a powerful sign that you be telepathic.

LET ME GIVE YOU AN EXAMPLE. When I was a child I a lot of times used to walk back home from school by a RIVER on the way home. One night I saw a NIGHTMARE, which I saw a man who was cycling alongside me on the road, lose balance and fall into the river. I was terrified of the fact that this was actually happening that I was skeptic about EVEN going to school that day. Yet, I went to the school, MAKING MYSELF BELIEVE THAT I was only dreaming. Surprised to the core as I walked to my home that day I was shocked to see that A MAN WAS DRIVING A CYCLE IN DIRECT VIEW OF me, heading towards that ROAD RIGHT NEXT TO the river. I was unable to stop myself from stopping him and telling him not to ride his bike However, I did suggest that he walk along the ROAD , as it might be slippery. My feelings were further strengthened when we both realized that unexpectedly that road was extremely slippery, and an accident could have easily occurred if I had not warned him.

The thing about TELEPATHY is that it is frequently dismissed by adults as a mere whist. But that's not the situation with CHILDREN. They don't neglige such innate thoughts and they act upon them even though they haven't been conditioned by society to always think in a certain way.

* Dreams and Telepathy The world of dreams is one of the most intriguing things to have ever existed. The ways our unconscious and subconscious mind functions is an element that is intriguing as well as among the most difficult things we humans can examine and understand. While asleep the frequencies of our minds are more open and our brain waves are open to the reception of any data that our conscious mind could not have been able to handle otherwise. This is why telepathy is much with the state of dreams that we humans experience. In our dreams that most of the time we get a great deal of telepathic messages. However, the majority often is that when we awake and our brain doesn't consider it as real, ignoring the dream as just a figment of imagination which don't have any foundation.

The thing we need to realize is that time is not linear, unlike what we would like to believe. It is a cycle where OUR past, future and OUR present are all interconnected And EACH event has a connection with a different event. It might not appear to be connected to a specific moment in time but it is certain that it is connected with events in OUR past or in OUR future. Every word we speak and every thought We think of, and every emotion we experience are connected TOGETHER in a circle that plays its own game. AS A RESULT OF THAT, MANY A TIME, OUR TELEPATHIC POWERS START ACTING IN OUR DREAMS, GIVING US PRIOR IDEAS ABOUT THINGS YET TO HAPPEN. If you have recurring DREAMS, it is better to think about and analyze them rather than ignore them.

* Feelings that occur in your Third Eye Do you experience strange sensations around the middle of your forehead? Or do you notice a sharp pain in the area of your eye? You'll be amazed to learn that, contrary to the way we usually interpret this is a sign that it's connected to an eye issue that we suffer from, or migraine, this could be a sign that you possess telepathic powers. This location that we have mentioned is where the third eye is and is

considered to be an extremely vital chakra points that we have in our body.

Therefore, we presume that THIS area is aching at TIMES or displaying a TINGLING sensation. In that case, the chances are that your third eye is growing or you are developing TELEPATHIC capabilities. You must realize that you must accept your real-world reality and not shy away from it. If you choose to do it, the art of living is completely up to you. But before that, you must be aware of what it is. So, IF you accept this and acknowledge the truth about yourself, this pain will be automatically subsided.

"You are Empathetic You are Empathetic. Some people get confused about what Telepathy is in relation to what Empathy is, because they're very similar to each other. We all know that empathy is the ability people have to feel deeply what the other person feels or going through and telepathy occurs the state of having a keen perception of what is happening in the mind of another person. If we are able to think clearly it is not identical, but they share a lot in common. Both handle the thoughts and emotions of others, and are able to comprehend exactly what they are experiencing.

IF YOU ARE AN EMPATH, YOU WILL OBVIOUSLY HAVE THESE DEEP FEELINGS OF UNDERSTANDING FOR OTHER PEOPLE'S NEEDS, THEIR CHARACTER IN GENERAL FOR YOU TO KNOW WHAT THEY ARE GOING THROUGH AND TO GET A PRIOR UNDERSTANDING OF WHAT STEPS THEY MIGHT TAKE NEXT GIVEN YOU UNDERSTAND HOW THEIR MIND WORKS. They are VERY SIMILAR to HOW the mind of a PERSON who HAS TELEPATHIC abilities, thinks. It could also HAPPEN that the EMPATHETIC powers in you give rise to TELEPATHIC powers over a certain duration of time.

Connection with Spirit World Spirit World - Many a time, it happens that a person who has psychic abilities isn't fully awake to the truth due to a variety of reasons or ways of disorientation. However, even if you've not been awake to the truth, you should consider certain questions such as whether you find yourself drawn to your spiritual self frequently or if you experience an intense sense of connection to your family members. Are you able to feel a sense of comfort and peace when you engage in mindfulness or meditation? One of the strongest explanations for this is that you are telepathic and have abilities that remain being discovered. The reason for this is that your internal consciousness recognizes the truth about yourself and in your being and these are only indications of it that assist you in becoming awake to your true self.

* Picking up Lies Have you noticed that you can quickly discern whether you know someone is in fact lying? If yes it could be a indicator that you may be telepathic. Telepathic individuals can easily feel an impression in their stomachs of something that hasn't occurred yet, or when something is not natural and doesn't work the manner it's meant to be. Telepathic

people are born with this characteristic their brains to communicate with their mind which makes it easier to detect people who are lying. The fact that something is not natural and that the person in question is hiding something can easily be discerned by people who are telepathic since the normal frequency begins being altered.

Chapter 13: Abuse Of Emotions Is Not Ok How To Identify And Protect Yourself From This Abuse.

Sexual Abuse is Not Permitted or accepted.

There are times when women in long-term relationships may not be aware that they are being victimized.

Nat with all of his flaws and negative emotions might believe that he's the best thing since bread sliced, and others around him may be thinking the same however, he's no emotional abuser. Sometimes, it is just the case that emotional abusers are lively and vivacious, but it is typically to conceal their desire to harming others close to them. If an emotional abuser had been at a party hosted by Nat or Rath it would have been completely different. Abusers should be afraid for when their partners/colleagues/etc. are fighting against their manipulation of emotions. A battlefield of emotions isn't a secure place for anyone, much less the victim. Victim is a demeaning phrase, (thanks society and social media) therefore, from this point on, they'll be referred to as winners. I can imagine that this could get confusing if you've known a Viktor and you think of him each time you think of him, but keep in mind the next chapter is going to be a bit serious.

As the emotional abuser, similar to the roles of empaths and narcissists in the previous chapters, Abs will be the same as Abs himself. The guy (well I hope not) who plays Mr. Right, only for every reason that isn't good enough. He lives in the most perfect house and an ideal car and and the perfect lifestyle. However, his life at home isn't ideal because his spouse and family members living in the house are struggling under his sway. The worst part is that the person who is suffering from it may not even realize or don't want to consider that his abuse of emotions is still an act of abuse. If you're forced to conceal it with makeup or a scarf or even a lie, that's abusing and the people (and ladies) who abuse their emotions must be on guard. It's important to note that I'm using the terms "you" and "the victor in this chapter interchangeably. Victors could be anyone you know or even yourself, thus the use of the terms in a similar way (I believe) can help restore some of the autonomy that is lacking in their personal lives.

Abs believes that he is amazing however, even if he admits that he's an abuser, what's the point? Emotional abuse and its consequences are not as evident as sexual or physical violence, and Abs can use this advantage to the fullest extent. Abs does this to his spouse so that it can keep them in a fearful state when they are away from home or at work. This means that the partner is unaware that they're being emotionally abused and accept the abuse as aspect of life. The most important thing to keep in mind in addressing emotional abuse, is that you know the nature of it and why abusers resort to it. Abs will not be able to explain it to you what to do, so let me to speak for myself.

As was discussed in the earlier chapters, control can energize the perpetrator and Abs utilizes the control he enjoys to gain more. Abs is after everything and wants it now. This is to ensure the control and subordination of the most common their sexual or romantic partners, however, coworkers as well as family members may also be targeted. It can have long-lasting consequences and many victims never recover. It's a bleak reality and I'm so sorry. Affects the self-esteem of the women or women affected; it affects their relationships with other people as many are scared of repeatedly abused people. Repression that they experience tarnish their character, preventing the winner to view them as anything other than an innocent victim. The cycle of abuse and manipulation persists until something is done similar to a washer that repeats the same load of delicates, hour after hour. The abuse of emotions can be the start of other types of abuse. Observing the signs can assist anyone you're with, saving their lives.

It is important to be aware of the Signs, so you can Find Assistance.

There are some indicators of emotional abuse. Abs may employ any of the strategies to control the situation and the female who is involved. The initial signs of emotional abuse include humiliation, denial, and criticism. In high school, getting named names was normal, but when you are someone who is in an intimate relationship the possibility of being called names are indicators of emotional abuse. These are usually coupled with cruel or derogatory names for pets. Pet names can be adorable but if your partner refers to you as "tiger-striped (referring to stretch marks)"chubby angel" instead of 'angel' the wording is appropriate. An adorable name shouldn't contain a hint of hurt. An endearing name could also be a vulgar name that you won't use in public. These names are acceptable when you wish they to appear. The key difference is your agreement in using the names.

Character assassination isn't just a thing that happens only in Game of Thrones, and even though your character's assassination may not include swords or dragons however, it is more damaging to your mental well-being. Character assassination can be used as strategy to make the person who wins think they're not a good person. The internalization of abuse may have long-lasting emotional consequences. The shouting, the jokes, and patronizing might seem silly at first, since everyone shouts and makes bad personal jokes about their buddies, isn't it? Abs and Nat often do this often. Wrong. The person who's on the other isn't one to be yelled at, and being the center of the jokes everyone else is or hearing that you failed, but it's not their fault that they failed. That's the way they are. There's no consolation prize for those who are the victims of emotional abuse. Abs definitely won't give you one.

People don't like to argue in public. It's awkward. It's not a good idea to let anyone be aware of your delicates that have been sat with wash cycles that are repeated Fighting in public is usually regarded as unprofessional by those who observe. Abs does not care and often picks fights with others to make the person who is being ridiculed uncomfortable to respond. If their goal is to manage the other person, is there a better method to manage the amount of humiliation their partner suffers? It could be the sole way that the winner reaches out to the abuser to seek comfort after an incredibly painful experience in the public.

On the opposite end on the other hand, dismissiveness can another sign of abuse. If your partner/friend/family member dismisses your achievements or goals, they could be an emotional abuser, using this tactic until something is done to stop them. Another time, that washing machine. I'm hoping it's a great model, because it's going need to put lots of things on repeat. Sarcasm can cause a conflict of opinion to those who listen to it. Some people believe it's true that "sarcasm is the most superior kind of intelligence" however, others view it for what it truly is an effective method to hide a snarky attitude. The people who claim they don't realize how sarcasm affects an individual. Tone plays a significant role in the way words are taken into impact, and even if the words appear innocent, the way they are delivered can be brutal. Partner such as Abs who use sarcasm typically reduce the severity when confronted, saying that the winner is sensitive and should not take it so seriously.

Conclusion

As as promised, you will receive various tools that can aid you through all the encounters you'll encounter dealing with the energy vampires. As an empath, you've got lots of emotions to manage and this is an opportunity you'll learn to be grateful for. Energy vampires can cause some harm, but you have the knowledge to safeguard yourself from their destructive ways and even their abusive methods. It's now possible for you to feel the emotions that you experience and even the ones that are difficult. There aren't many people who experience the same way you do and this is the reason you are a distinct person. The ability to discern the thoughts and emotions of other people is unique Don't believe that this isn't true.

People who are emotionally vulnerable. This is why it is normal to have no issue being open about your feelings with other people. This is often to energy-hungry person's advantage because they thrive on overcoming others. However, this can make you feel like you are a constantly targeted person to target. Naturally, this is uncomfortable and difficult to deal with, especially if you're already struggling with other aspects of your life. It's normal to be a victim of this since you think it's what you deserve however, this behavior isn't necessary to endure. It is possible to break free of the cycle by speaking for yourself and protecting your vital energy.

There is always a solution when your life seems overwhelming. Once you have identified the ways you're being treated and how you are being treated, you can take the energy vampire out of your body to stop having to suffer any more suffering. This isn't easy to do, particularly when you are you are dealing with a abusive partner however, you can conquer it. Through implementing your self-care routine and separating yourself from people who only provide negative energy, you'll be able to see how keeping your unique abilities as an empath be very relaxing and satisfying. When you keep an eye for possible energy vampires it is possible to sort out the people that are currently draining your energy. Keep in mind that they're only trying to take your money. They don't have the ability to give you your respect that you merit. If you do not want to share all of your vulnerableness, you don't need to. This is something that you are able to choose.

The best way to stay away from being a victim is to concentrate on you. Make this a starting base for a new age of self-love. You're able to love and take care of other people, but it's time to focus your attention back to you. If you concentrate on your task your energy vampires will get bored because you're not triggering the response they are desperate for. They seek attention and recognition for what they do and say, and are usually obsessive. If they can see that you're not bothered by their actions They will most likely pass on and move on to another person who responds.

Empaths are regarded as some of the most knowledgeable and fascinating people. Remember this next time you are wondering the reason you feel everything deeply. You aren't "too too" and "too emotionally." What you've got is a heightened sensitivity to everything happening in the world around you. When you are watching these events the brain processes them as if experiencing them all. The ability to put yourself in someone else's positions is your skill even if you aren't intending to.

This book can be used to assist you when you feel overwhelmed or depressed. Reading through any of the information and these guidelines can keep you aware that you're not all on your own. Thank you so much for reading and don't forget to leave a review that is positive! Do not forget that you are surrounded by amazing people and they'll provide you with greatness.

www.ingramcontent.com/pod-product-compliance
Lightning Source LLC
Chambersburg PA
CBHW071837080526
44589CB00012B/1024